Letters from Normandy

Letters from Normandy

JOHN MERCER

AMBERLEY

To my wife Olive,
without whom this book would never have been finished.

First published 2010

Amberley Publishing
Cirencester Road, Chalford,
Stroud, Gloucestershire GL6 8PE

www.amberley-books.com

British Library Cataloguing in Publication Data.
A catalogue record for this book is available from the British Library.

ISBN 978-1-4456-0176-2

Typeset in 10.5pt on 13pt Sabon.
Typesetting and Origination by Amberley Publishing.
Printed in the UK.

Contents

Military portrait of the author, taken before the Normandy landings.

Introduction

I found these letters in an envelope marked 'Family'. They were written over the period from June 1944 until the end of the war in 1945. There were other letters, which have not been preserved. The earliest letters would have been subject to censorship by my troop commander. Those preserved were not censored, and the special envelopes in which they were sent were introduced later in the Normandy campaign. The letters that remain are linked to the War Diary of 185 Field Regiment Royal Artillery, and when that regiment was disbanded in December 1944, the author was transferred to a special unit of the 7th Armoured Division. This was the Counter Mortar Officer's Staff (CMOS). From the date of that transfer the letters are linked to the War Diary of that unit. War Diaries were kept by all regiments. As far as the artillery was concerned, each battery had a clerk – a bombardier or a gunner – whose task it was to record all incoming messages other than fire orders, and to log daily events. Sometimes several days at a time would be logged together. The battery diaries would be inspected by a battery officer and passed on to the regimental headquarters, where they would be edited and written up by another officer. It could be the colonel himself or one delegated by him. The regimental diaries have been preserved and are now at the National Archives at Kew, where they are available for inspection and copying. During the war, and for some time afterwards, these were secret documents.

A Bren Carrier passes a knocked-out German tank in Rauray. (*Imperial War Museum*, B6137)

CHAPTER ONE

Before Normandy

I was born in 1923 to Leonard John Mercer, an electrical buyer, and Daisie Emma Mercer (née Weaving). I was an only child. An older brother had died in the influenza epidemic following the First World War. I spent most of my childhood in Bexleyheath, Kent, and attended a private grammar school. Aged seventeen I entered the Sidcup branch of Barclays Bank as a junior clerk on a salary of £1 a week. On 15 September 1940 my father, an air raid warden, was killed by a bomb jettisoned from a crashing Dornier. He was a post warden in the Air Raid Precautions, later to be called the Civil Defence Force. There was a large public air raid shelter close to where we lived. The sirens sounded at 2 p.m., and taking our dinners with us we went to the shelter to be at hand if needed. I suppose there were about twelve people in the shelter. My father went outside to usher in passengers from a trolleybus that had stopped by the shelter, as the fighting overhead presaged danger. As my father was leading people in from the trolleybus, the Dornier jettisoned one of its bombs, which landed in the road, wrecking the trolleybus and throwing my father and two passengers into the entrance of the shelter. I was still in the shelter, and seeing the entrance filled with smoke and debris I opened the escape hatch and helped those within to get out. There was the noise of more bombs, and fighting overhead. Spent cartridges from the fighter fire clattered onto the road like heavy rain. I did not recognise my father at first; he looked like a dirty bundle, lying where someone had left a jumble of old clothes. The two others hurt by the blast were staggering to their feet, one badly wounded, with a useless broken arm. I recognised the bundle to be my father. He was unconscious, with a hole in his white helmet and a deep gash in his head. As an ambulance arrived I heard him breathe his last. The ambulance leader was a family friend. 'Jesus Christ!' he said.

The author and his father in the garden in Bexleyheath, 1933.

My father was taken to the Brook Hospital in Woolwich, where my mother and I went to identify him. He looked surprised. He was buried in Crayford churchyard. We had asked for a bugler, as my father had been in the Royal Flying Corps in the First World War. We were told that the only bugler available had been sent to play the 'Last Post' for the German aircrew who had crashed the Dornier on Barnehurst Golf Course. As you can imagine, that did not please my mother. As the vicar intoned the funeral liturgy, the siren sounded again. I still regularly visit my father's grave and endeavour with the help of my wife to keep it tidy. I hope my son, who is a parish priest, will do the same. Local residents got up a petition asking that my father be awarded a medal for gallantry, but this was rejected. His name was placed on the war memorial at Crayford Manor House, but his initials were incorrectly carved. The same week came news that my Uncle Walter, a sheep farmer on the Isle of Sheppey, had also been killed.

That winter my mother and I sought refuge in Wraysbury, Buckinghamshire, staying with a distant relative. I was transferred to the

The author and his mother in the garden in Wraysbury, 1941.

Ashford branch of the bank in Middlesex, and worked there until my call-up in June 1942. My mother later became a paid air raid warden in neighbouring Staines. Another relative, whom I had only once met, left me £500 in his will. With that we were able to take out a mortgage on a bungalow in Wraysbury, and my mother was able to augment her income by taking in a lodger. I joined the Home Guard until the regular Army claimed me.

Wraysbury was and still is a sprawling village beside the Thames. Many of its residents worked in London and commuted every day. They were in the main bankers, insurance officials and civil servants. Those who worked locally were postmen, shopkeepers, gravel pit workers or workers in transport. The Home Guard Company was formed of such men, with the addition of some retired men. I was its youngest member at eighteen. Its captain was Lt Sawyer, who had served in the regular Army at some time. There were three sergeants; one was a senior bank official, one a self-employed cartoonist. Our duties were to patrol the area every night on a rota basis. A retired bank official, Mr Fairweather, took a paternal interest in me. I was invited to tea with him and his wife. I think they were childless, and in view of my recent bereavement he saw me as the young son he never had. We had military exercises and a summer camp. We were shown how to kill silently, how to make Molotov cocktails, and how to shoot.

We practised infantry tactics. It was all taken very seriously. It was a lot of fun, too. I was thrilled to be able to fire a Ross rifle (0.303, Canadian, and a bit of a brute) at Bisley, and even more thrilled to be issued with a Remington 0.300 (American, and a delight to fire). I was given twenty rounds of ammunition to be taken home with the rifle and carefully stored in my wardrobe, and then to be taken out and meticulously cleaned on Sunday mornings before parade. We also had the excitement of having night manoeuvres in Windsor Great Park, and on one such occasion one of our sergeants put his hip out of joint. This caused some unkind merriment. Later in the year we were taken by coach to see Gracie Fields on the stage at a Watford cinema. This was on her return from America, and she was nervous about her reception. She need not have worried; everyone applauded her with enthusiasm. All this was to end when, after a medical and an interview at Hounslow, I was told that I had passed A1, and that I had been selected to be a signaller in the artillery. If recruits had been in the Home Guard they were told to keep their khaki uniforms when reporting to their designated units, but to change black leather gaiters for khaki web ones. On the train north I found myself in the company of another former Home Guard member, Wally Lipyeat.

Wraybury Home Guard, January 1942. The author is third from the left, middle row.

Learning to soldier in Scarborough

The train steamed out of Kings Cross through tunnels, causing thick black smoke to enter our compartment. Not for nothing was London known as The Smoke. I had never travelled out of Kings Cross before, and as the train puffed along I noticed all we passed with keen interest. We stopped in Peterborough and then at York, where there was another train to take us on a scenic route to Scarborough. I have never lost my interest in railways. I was bound for the 37th Signal Training Regiment, Royal Artillery, based in Burneston Barracks on the edge of the town. On arrival we were issued with khaki jackets and trousers, which had been impregnated with some anti-gas powder. The clothes smelt unpleasant and were stiff and ill-fitting. We were glad to be confined to barracks for the first month as we would have felt awkward walking in the town as obvious rookies. We collected canvas bags and filled them with straw to make palliasses, and slept on the polished barrack floor. We did not complain; we were in the Army now. The first month was spent in 'A' battery, learning to drill on the parade ground. We rehearsed over and over again falling into three ranks, slope arms, present arms, to the front salute, and so on. Our sergeant was unsmiling and painstaking. We called him 'Sergeant Got-it' as that was his continual expression of encouragement. He had a sidekick, a bombardier, who was viewed with some awe as he had been a professional footballer for Middlesborough. Those in the squad who followed football reported well of him.

In 'B' battery we learned to drive a variety of vehicles, including three-tonners and motorbikes. If the Army taught me nothing else it taught me how to drive in all kinds of weather. I did my final driving test on a Guy 15 cwt truck. It had five gears and double declutching; no intermesh gearing in that vehicle. It was a brute. In 'C' battery we learned about signalling: Morse code, wireless transmission, line laying. In order to qualify you had to be able to read Morse code transmitted at twelve words a minute. We never used it again, for in the field we always used radio.

I quite enjoyed my time in Scarborough. Drill could be tedious, but there was great satisfaction in working in a squad and getting near-perfect. I made good friends. We were all keen to be good soldiers. Most of us felt that the war had to be fought and won. Nearly all of us were from the south of England, and had been juniors in banking or insurance. We were grammar school kids. The highlight of the week was to go out on Friday evening, having received a week's pay, and have a couple of half-pints at the Balmoral. The Balmoral no longer exists, nor for that matter do Burneston barracks. My weekly pay was 14s a week, and of that I sent 9s home to my mother. I did not smoke then, and passed on my free cigarette issue to Geoff North, a new friend. He had been a junior in Lloyds bank, and his father the export manager for Whitbreads. Did I take any money for the cigarettes? I cannot remember, and I cannot ask Geoff because he died of a heart attack aged thirty-eight, many years ago. Another close friend was John Dyer. He could play the organ, and was assistant organist at a church in Petts Wood in Kent. His pleasure was to take Geoff and me around Nonconformist churches in Scarborough and play popular music on the organ. Since they were not Anglican churches, he did not feel he was being irreverent.

One night we were called out to put down a heath fire. Taken to the site on the moors by truck, we spent a warm night putting out the flames and smouldering bracken. It was a good exercise in working together. We regularly mounted guard by night, manning the beach defences, two by two. I remember one night on guard with Wally Coldrick looking at the wonderfully bright night sky, and contemplating with him the meaning of the universe. What were we in this great universe? Was there a God? This was not the only time I discussed such matters with others. I was to meet Wally twice again, once on a gun position in Holland and then again as a schoolmaster, years later, when he brought a team to play cricket at the school where I was then teaching. He taught art; I taught history. As far

'A' Troop 37 Signal Training Regiment, Scarborough. The author is fourth from the right, back row. Sergeant 'Got-it' is centre, front row.

as I can remember only two members of our squad were rejected. There was Jennings, a strange lad who did not communicate with anyone. He was discharged from the Army on the grounds of mental incapacity. Some wondered if had had 'worked his ticket'. Then there was Ernie Taylor, who was invalided out because wearing battledress gave him impetigo.

On completion of the course, Lt Fright, 'C' battery commander, a public schoolboy, met us for a meal, and we told him a bit about ourselves and he revealed his human side to us. A number of the squad were sent to a War Office Selection Board, and of these some were accepted for officer training. Rather to my surprise I was put forward to go to a WOSB. While waiting for this I watched most of my former colleagues depart to various units. A handful of us remained in the barracks and were engaged in maintaining the overhead signal lines around the town, and having 'tea and a wad' in the local NAAFI (the Navy, Army and Air Force Institute). Soon I was sent to the WOSB at Catterick, and while there I had the good fortune to meet my old schoolfriend Cecil Shefferd, who was in the Royal Corps of Signals, and was waiting to go abroad.

The course I was chosen to go on would lead to a commission in an anti-tank regiment. I had been given a week's home leave, and collected my travel warrant. Later in the evening I saw on Part Two Orders that the leave had been cancelled, and that I was to go the next day to the Pre-OCTU (Officer Cadet Training Unit), based in the woods of the North Downs above Wrotham. I was filled with dismay. I had not been home since June of the previous year. I told a friend that I had not seen the notice and early next morning set off home. I did not get very far. I was arrested by two military policemen at York as I got off the train, and was sent back to the barracks. Major Harding, the senior commander, saw me the next day. He was a soldier of the old school, but a charming man. He was not charming on this occasion. One of his men had spoiled his record as a commanding officer. How dare I play the fool, with him! I am afraid I lied through my teeth: I had not seen the Part Two Orders. He said that he had information from one of my squad that I had. I maintained my innocence. He affirmed that he would get to the bottom of the matter, and dismissed me. But I heard no more, and armed with a fresh travel warrant, I set off for Wrotham. How I had hoped to get away with my illegal journey I do not know. It was anger that sent me, but contrition that brought me back. I had asked for compassionate leave on my arrival at the camp. I stressed that my mother was a lonely widow and I needed to see her. I was given three days, and on my return I fell foul of the troop commander who was taking us through the course. He did not like me at all, and filed an adverse report to accompany me to the OCTU at Ilkley, in Yorkshire. I knew nothing of this until I was interviewed and was returned to the ranks after failing to meet the required physical standard. This was a blow to my pride, but in retrospect I realised I was not mature enough to make the grade. I was not happy at Ilkley. I felt I was a misfit.

From Larkhill to London

I think the War Office did not know what to do with me. I was sent to Larkhill, the Royal Artillery base on Salisbury Plain. I remember attending a church service and being strangely moved by the liturgy, and I walked some miles to Stonehenge in a flurry of snow in May. I was then moved to Watford, to a holding regiment. We were sleeping in empty houses in bunks. I knew no one. I consoled myself by forcing myself to smoke. I found the first two or three cigarettes unpalatable, but with persistence I developed a smoking habit, which when in Normandy had risen to forty a day. I hasten to add that I stopped completely in 1961.

There was a second consolation. I was only twenty miles from Wraysbury, so with a twenty-four-hour pass I could go home. I brought my bicycle back with me, and after that I could steal away, ensuring that a colleague spoke up for me at roll call. I also met a very pretty girl, but it did not last long, as I was posted to a field regiment stationed in Newcastle, and regraded as a battery clerk. Our unit was using Blaydon Race Course, sleeping in hutments. The tram took you into Newcastle, and I was made welcome by members of a Methodist Church and invited to the home of one of its members. The daughter of the family was also very attractive and we became friends, but not for long, as the regiment was given two weeks embarkation leave. I returned unexpectedly to Wraysbury, wondering where we would be going abroad. Would it be Italy or would it be Burma? We hoped it would not be Burma. We were lined up on the quayside ready to embark when an officer called me out of the ranks. 'You are not going with this unit. I have just received a telegram. You have another War Office Selection Board.' So my new mates sailed away without me, and I was posted yet again to an unknown destination. When I was called again for the WOSB, I asked to be taken off the list of candidates. I did not want to be commissioned and risk failure again. I suspect I was given a second board because of my treatment at the end of the Wrotham course. Someone had looked over my papers and thought I still had promise. But as far as I was concerned I did not want to be commissioned. I was posted to 274 Battery of 185 Field Regiment stationed in Motherwell, Scotland. The regiment was part of the 49th West Riding Infantry Division, nicknamed the Polar Bears because it had served for two years defending Iceland.

I had an interesting train journey from Newcastle to Carlisle through the border country; then there was a change of train before I reached Motherwell. I began in the battery office. In that role I made a friend from another battery, on the telephone. This was Maurice Tyerman, also a signaller, who had followed after me at the Signal Training Regiment, and like me had became a battery clerk. We soon met, and I persuaded him to revert to signalling, which he did. We shall hear more of Maurice later. He was to become a lifelong friend. I had been pressured to leave the battery office by Denis Bould, a lance bombardier, who befriended me on my arrival at Motherwell. He taught me to play chess using a pocket set. Surely a hard way to begin chess, but it served me in good stead, and I played chess after the war for many years. After a short instruction and testing, I was upgraded to driver/operator, and when the regiment moved to Suffolk it began preparing for the Normandy landings as part of 70th Infantry Brigade of the 49th West Riding (Polar Bear) Division. We were stationed initially in large empty houses and bungalows in the Suffolk village of Walberswick. Among my memories is making my way in the dark across heathland to Maurice Tyerman's billet, and falling headlong into a deep anti-tank ditch. I emerged shaken but unharmed. At his billet we read poetry by the flickering light of a wood fire. He had studied for two years at a teacher-training college, and I warmed to him immediately. He widened my outlook and my understanding of prose and poetry. Not long after that, we moved to Sheringham, on the north Norfolk coast. It was from there that we set off for London on D-Day, 6 June.

Fd Mar. Bernard Montgomery.

274 Battery was a Leeds territorial unit. Its members had served in Iceland and were a friendly and loyal bunch of chaps. There were a few southerners already in the battery, but essentially its officers and men were from the Leeds area. A new friend was George Newson. He came up the stairs to the room in the requisitioned house where I was sleeping, and dumped his kitbag on a spare bed. He had just been posted to us from the South Notts Hussars. We took to each other immediately, and he was soon introduced to my other close friends, Maurice Tyerman and Dennis Bould. Although we were in Sheringham for only a few weeks, we went to the cinema a number of times and shared our pleasure in watching Bing Crosby and Laurel and Hardy. I acquired several nicknames, usually invented by George: Johnny Mercer (after the American songwriter); Johann; Mer; Pinocchio (I do not have a long nose, but I suppose I was always curious).

You may have gained from this chapter that I was quite innocent, naïve even, but able to stand on my own feet. Coming from a close family, devoted to my widowed mother, it is strange that I never felt homesick. My letters home reflect this naïvety, and my care for my mother. I had recently lost my father, and my mother had lost her husband. It was not unnatural that we had a very close affinity. Reading the letters after these sixty-five years, they seem mawkish at times, but that was how it was to me in those distant days.

From the War Diary, 16 February 1944:
Entire Regiment paraded at Sprowston Hall, Norwich, for a visit of the new C-in-C General Sir B. L. Montgomery KCB DSO.

I recall lining up with the three batteries (274, 191, 386) in a large field and waiting for what seemed like forever. Then Monty arrived in a Jeep and we were called to attention. Monty climbed onto the bonnet and told all of us to break ranks and crowd round him. He harangued us in his inimitable way, with his rather high, raspy voice, exuding confidence and telling us what we would be up against. He told us that we would win. I felt he gave me confidence, and although I never saw him again, I have always thought that his many critics did not realise his charisma with the rank and file. He might have been arrogant, a know-all and difficult to his colleagues, especially with our American allies, but he was a great military leader.

From the War Diary, 27 April 1944:
Regt moved to Gorleston to parade with other units of Divisional Artillery for inspection by His Majesty the King.

I remember lining the road, one of hundreds of soldiers spaced out as far as the eye could see. Eventually the King drove slowly by in a car. He was gone in a few moments. I was concerned to see his face staring out of the window, showing thick make-up. He must have been a sick man, but we did not know it at the time.

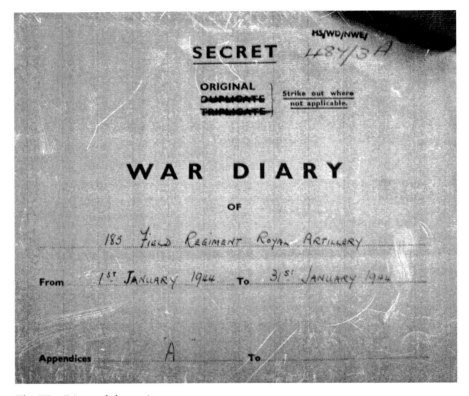

The War Diary of the regiment.

CHAPTER TWO

Normandy

From the War Diary, 8 June 1944:
All ranks briefed in the operational role of the regt. Vehicles only moved from marshalling area (Woodford, Essex) to docks to load onto two ships required to accommodate the regt. for the voyage.

We left Sheringham on D-Day, driving through the night to a park in Woodford. After a couple of hours it was my turn to drive, taking over from Dennis Bould. Try as I could, I was unable to get the Chevrolet truck moving. It jumped the clutch every time. The truck was so heavily laden and waterproofed that I lacked the skill to drive it. To my chagrin Dennis had to take over the wheel. In the early hours of 7 June we pulled into our camp. We were briefed by our troop commander, Captain Thomson, in a packed tent. We were to be the follow-up division, taking over from the 50th Division, which was making the initial landing on 'Gold' beach. The aim of the invading force was to drive for Mount Pinson, some twenty miles inland.

From the War Diary, 9-16 June:

12	Advance Party lands in theatre of operations.
13-15	Ships anchored off bridgehead. Period of unloading ships and landing the regt.
14-15	Vehs landed and de-waterproofed and, as available, moved into action area North of DOUX SAINTE MARGUERITE.
16	Regt·in action and engaged on barrage in support of 146 bde attack on CRISTOT.
	Regt supported attack by 147 Inf Bde with smoke screen and barrage on PARC DE BOISLONDE.

Regt fired concentrations on call from rep with 70 Inf Bde
for attack on Sainte Pierre. Attack successful.
Further concentrations at call provided by regt to meet
German left flank thrusts.

I was on a Liberty ship[1] crossing the English Channel. We left the London
docks and went downriver at night. When we rounded the Kent coast and
entered the English Channel, we were given a smokescreen to hide us from
the view of German guns at Cap Gris Nez. It was an uneasy hour. All
troops were ordered below to their quarters to stand by their hammocks.
However nothing happened and we proceeded to sail along the coast quite
close in, protected by motor torpedo boats. As darkness fell we turned
south and began to head for France. I was doing night watch in the early
hours of the morning when I saw a ship approaching with bright lights.
I stared at in disbelief. What was such an illuminated ship doing in the
middle of a war? Such a target! Then I realised it was a hospital ship sailing
back to England with wounded men on board. It was a shining target for
an enemy submarine, but by having bright lights and Red Cross markings
it hoped to be allowed a safe passage. As far as I know, it did.

Dawn brought an incredible sight. There were many, many ships off the
coast of Normandy. Out at sea there were battleships, which from time to
time fired a great broadside at a target inland, filling the air with a clang
like the shutting of a great steel door. Destroyers drove through the sea,
the 'whoop–whoop' of their sirens clearly audible. There were numerous
smaller vessels ferrying men and supplies ashore, and far out to sea coming
behind our ship were tugs pulling strange blocks of concrete on rafts.
What could these be for? Later we learned that they were components of
the Mulberry Harbour to be placed in position out to sea to provide an
artificial harbour. Our ship anchored, and we stayed at the anchorage for
several days. The initial landings had gone well and we were not needed
as early as anticipated. The weather improved and we spent the days on
deck chatting, smoking and reading. I was reading a book by George
Orwell called *Burmese Days*. I finished it before we went ashore. We were
undisturbed by the enemy during the day. We had achieved command of the
air, and the V-1s that Hitler had started to launch were directed at London,
and not at our Normandy landings. In fact we knew nothing of the V-1s
until much later. Had Hitler directed his 'buzz bombs' onto the beaches,
the great invasion might have been a disaster. At night the Luftwaffe came
over and carried out bombing raids. On our ship we had some multiple
'pom-poms', which were known as Chicago Pianos. Each gun consisted
of six barrels that were fired simultaneously, causing an unmistakable
racket. When all the nearby ships were firing, the din was incredible. We

had spent fragments from shells fired by other ships landing on the deck, but the German pilots failed to do any damage to us. However, some ships were less lucky, and at least one of our destroyers was sunk.

At last it was our turn to come ashore. Large floating rafts known as 'Rhinos', like enormous Meccano creations and propelled by outboard engines, pulled alongside us, manned by marines. The trucks and guns were winched over the side to be gently lowered onto the rafts. Load after load were despatched ashore. Then it was the turn of the command staff, the signallers and OP assistants.[2] We climbed down a rope ladder with our weapons slung over our shoulders. It was quite a tricky thing to do. The Rhino rose up and down with the swell of the sea, and the current moved the raft a foot or two away from the ship's side, so each of us in turn had to judge just when to jump from the bottom of the rope ladder in order to land safely on the Rhino. We all managed it successfully. For some reason I remember making two trips using the ladder.

Our trucks had been waterproofed to enable us to be driven from the raft into the water. I suppose we could safely drive off into two feet of water. The driver had to keep the engine running and not use the clutch pedal lest water ran into the exhaust pipe and into the engine. It had been well rehearsed in England. None of the vehicles foundered, but one of our bombardiers missed his footing and splashed into the sea. There was a great shout of mirth, more relief of nervous tension than amusement. We were ashore.

I was in a GPO truck,[3] designated GA1. L/Bdr Bould was the driver. Beside him was Lt Cannell, the GPO. Beside me in the back was Fred Dalton, the OP assistant. There were two other officers in 'A' troop. Our troop was commanded by Capt. Thomson, who rode in a Bren carrier,[4] and was the forward position officer to direct the fire orders. Lt Small was the troop leader who travelled in another OP truck, designated GA2. He was the junior officer, there to work with Lt Cannell at the command post. He too had a signaller and a GPO assistant in the back of the truck, and a driver beside him. The two drivers were also signallers. Signallers who were also drivers were promoted to be driver/operators and were classed as Army tradesmen. Capt. Thomson had a driver/assistant and two signallers. By a strange training omission, no driver/operators had been trained to drive a Bren carrier. This was a tracked vehicle and therefore quite a different animal to handle. Had our Bren driver been incapacitated there would not have been another driver.

We drove off the beach. Sitting in the back of GA1 all I could see was sand, and the occasional piece of wreckage. A vast dust cloud began to envelop our convoy as we left the beach. The sand dunes gave way to a tarmac road, with fields and woods on each side. After a little while our truck drove into a meadow and stopped. At once I began to tune the radio to our network. The 22 set radio had a limited range, at best five miles. Our net had a limited air space. So many radios were in use and each net was individually tuned for purpose. The radio band was changed frequently so that the enemy should not become accustomed to the authenticity of one network. The control set was at battery level, but it could be linked to regimental level, which in turn could be linked to divisional level and even further. Most of our targets were regimental targets, called in radio terms 'Mike', so when the OP was given a target by the infantry company, the troop commander would identify the target and the signaller at the OP end would call, 'Mike target, Mike target, Mike target.' The signaller at the GPO end would repeat and pass on the necessary gunnery information so that the guns would be brought to bear on the invisible target. This was known as indirect fire, for rarely were the gun members required to fire over open sights at an enemy close enough to be seen. Once the net was established the radios would be manned day and night, signallers taking shifts. I suppose I spent ten hours a day for five months listening on the radio, with only a break when out of the line, which was rare. Sometimes, if a battle was raging and there was no other signaller available, the ten hours on the radio might stretch to twelve or even longer. Looking back to those Normandy days my chief recollection is of being always tired, tired from loss of sleep exacerbated by periods of fear. There was never any time for boredom. My ears were filled with the buzz of the radio, the sound of harmonics, other interference, and the frequent call for a target.

We spent our first night somewhere in farmland a few miles inland. We were dog-tired and as soon as we had fed, we settled down for the night. I lay under the stars. The firmament of heaven shone and winked above me. I wondered again at the mystery of the night sky, untrammelled by street lighting. I had learned to love the dark during my Home Guard patrols. Darkness was my dear friend; I could see and not be seen. As I lay there happy to be safely landed after fearing death on the beaches, I relaxed. It was amazing; we were here in France and all in one piece! But where was the enemy? There was no sound of war. There were thousands of German soldiers within walking distance, but not within hearing. Nothing was happening. There was no sound of anything apart from a colleague's snore.

My reverie did not last long. Over the beaches shells began bursting, flashes of red disturbing the peace of the night sky. The noise of the explosions followed: a familiar sound. German aircraft were strafing the beaches, as they had done on previous nights. The shell bursts came closer overhead and soon the sound of enemy aircraft filled the sky. As the shell bursts chased the bombers, the shell splinters began to fall all around our encampment. Bits of hot shrapnel plopped into the grass. I quickly slithered under the nearest vehicle and banged my head on the differential. But this would have to do. It was not safe under the stars any more, and within a few moments I was fast asleep.

We did not have long to wait before an engagement (see the previous War Diary, 14-15 June). The guns were unhooked, the quads[5] sent to the rear, the command post established and the aiming post set up. Lt Cannell and his two assistants were at the gunnery board, the gun aimers had aligned their dial sites, and the signaller received the first fire orders. It was a troop target. The guns followed the fire orders and the gun sergeants reported that each gun was ready and awaited the order to fire.

'Fire!' came the cry. The troop[6] fired, and immediately there was an explosion that coincided with the firing of the guns. 'Cease firing!'

What had happened? Had the enemy got our range already? No, Sgt Gawler's gun had fired its first shell and hit a tree twenty feet in front of it. He had failed to check for crest clearance. The explosion sent a shower of shell splinters over the gun crew. Most were protected by the gun shield, but Stan Dickinson, a young gun number who had recently joined the troop, lay badly wounded by the gun limber. Dickinson was carried away by field ambulance and we never saw him again. He was shipped back to England and remained in hospital for some months, and when discharged was rated unfit for active service and was relegated to home service. After the war he was to become a senior civil servant. I met him years later; he had discovered the existence of the 274 Battery Annual Reunion in Leeds long before I did. Being from Chorley in Lancashire, he was able to slip over into Yorkshire quite easily. As he had missed the Normandy campaign he was eager to find out what had happened to his former unit, and had taken research seriously, going to Kew to trace the War Diary, and joining the Normandy Veterans Association. Since meeting him in Leeds in 1992, I have maintained a yearly correspondence with him.

Not long after this incident we moved our gun position to an orchard near the village of Audrieu. We were just moving in, the guns had been allocated positions, and the command post was being set up under a tree. I was not duty signaller, and helped set up the command post. I had just begun to dig down to give the post protection when over the air we heard fire orders giving directions. The range was decreasing rapidly. The enemy was launching a counter-attack. Spent tank shells from enemy tanks whizzed through the orchard. Our troop sergeant-major, Beckwith, was hit, and was sitting on the ground cursing loudly and nursing his injured leg. His injury was far from superficial and he did not return to us until we were in Belgium some months later.

The order came: '800 yards; open sites.' Our gun crews prepared to fire their limited supplies of armour-piercing shells directly at enemy tanks as soon as they appeared. Some of our infantrymen ran out of the woods ahead, looking fearfully behind them. The gun crews stood steadily behind the limited protection of their gun shields. Lt Cannell and his assistants still sat under an apple tree looking unhappy and vulnerable. We all craned our necks, expecting the German tanks to break out of the wood ahead. The shells stopped whizzing, and the rattle of small arms fire died away. Silence reigned. It seemed that the attack had been halted and that the enemy had stabilised their forward positions about 1,500 yards ahead of us. News came that Jock Sims of 'B' troop had been killed in the next field. He was struck down as he carried a 25 lb shell to his gun. Poor Jock! He was a conscientious soldier, always turned out the smartest in the battery, always the first on parade to be the right marker.

Then we heard that Aston, the equipment repairer, was dead. Aston used to say, with a chuckle, how safe he was back at regimental headquarters, but this proved to be a false hope. He had jumped out of the back of a truck with his Sten submachine gun over his shoulder. The loaded magazine of 38 mm calibre bullets was in the gun, and as his feet touched the ground the shock of the impact triggered off the gun, and blew away the top of his head. Here was a lesson all had to learn. Never sling a Sten gun over your shoulder with a loaded magazine in position. Carry the magazine in a pouch or in a hip pocket, but never, never have it on the gun until you need to fire it. The Sten was a crude little submachine gun, made in numerous backyard workshops for about 7s (as the story went). Once the trigger was pulled, the heavy bolt flew back, inserting the new bullet and holding it in place by inertia just long enough to fire the round before being thrown back once more; so if the loaded gun was tapped on the ground, it would begin to fire of its own accord unless the safety catch was on. Even if it was in place, the vibration of any impact could dislodge it, and the gun would fire uncontrollably. Poor Aston. Poor Jock. Two dead and one injured so soon.

As quickly as possible we dug the command post well down and turned our attention to making ourselves safe. Fortunately the ground was easy to dig and George Newson[7] and I dug a trench, which we covered with branches and dead wood from the orchard, with earth piled on the top. We put our gas capes on the floor of the dugout and our blankets on top. It felt safe in our little hole. Not long after, we became aware of soldiers shuffling past. Some of our lads crowded out of the orchard to see what was happening. A long file of German soldiers, taken prisoner, clad in shabby mud-stained uniforms, were being marched back to the rear. They looked worn out and dispirited. Fred Dalton shouted out to them, 'Call yourself the master race! Look at you, you poor specimens, there's not a blonde Aryan among you!' Fred was not far wrong. These prisoners were mostly Poles and Russians who had been forced to join the German Army. They had put up a resistance on the beaches, but had been taken prisoner as the fighting moved inland.

We stayed on that gun position for about two weeks, our guns giving supporting fire day and night. Sometimes we were asked to put down a stonk[8] where the enemy was attacking. Sometimes we put down a barrage prior to our infantry advancing. Our range increased as our troops made gains.

There was one incident that affected us considerably. Captain Thomson was moving through the bocage[9] in the Bren carrier, standing up to see where he should go, when a sniper tied to a tree fired a burst of machine-gun fire. He fell, hit in the neck by three bullets, which wounded him grievously. Fortunately his carotid artery was unharmed. He was flown back to England and did not rejoin the troop until we were across the Seine. This meant that our troop had a series of officers transferred from other units in the regiment to act as our troop commander. Because the signaller with Thomson was also wounded and removed from the battle zone, a rota was set up so that those signallers at the command post would take it in turns to man the OP. In this way, I was up with the infantry for some time during the battle to capture the Rauray spur.

I vividly remember joining the OP for the first time. I was taken up through the bocage until the driver said he could go no further. I had two dags[10] to deliver to the carrier. It was a very hot day. I picked up one of the dags and started forward in the direction indicated by the Jeep driver. My route was through a narrow unploughed field surrounded on both sides by thick undergrowth. I was perspiring on account of the heat and because of fear. All was quiet, but there could be a sniper somewhere. The dag was heavy, and I had to stop from time to time to shift the weight. Eventually I reached the corner of the field, to see the carrier in a second narrow field. I dumped the dag and returned for the second one. I was easier in my mind this time, since my first journey had been uneventful.

A bizarre sight was before me. Sticking out of the top of the carrier's engine cowling were the fins of a large mortar bomb. The crew was resting on the ground. They had had a bad night of enemy mortaring. What was to be done? How could the bomb be dealt with? There was much animated discussion. Then the OP assistant, a bombardier whose name I have forgotten, climbed onto the carrier and very gently pulled the bomb from where it had landed. He climbed down with it in his hands and put it into the woods at the side of the field. We congratulated him. He took a great risk, but he had defused the situation. A little later an infantry officer consulted the troop commander and they decided to go as far forward as they deemed necessary to see what the enemy was up to. As the signaller,

I had to go with them with a No. 18 wireless set on my back to carry fire orders from the officer to the signaller left in the carrier. To take the carrier further forward on the recce would have given our position away. The No. 18 set had a limited range: just enough to carry messages to the carrier some 200 yards back. It was heavy and uncomfortable on the back. Any message I sent would be retransmitted via the carrier to the guns. I had to set up the radio net and adjust the volume.

We advanced cautiously to take a hidden position behind a bank. We could see German soldiers walking about. Some were washing. We could catch an occasional word or two. Our two officers conferred. I hoped they would not decide to fire on the Germans. They decided to leave them alone. Their position had been established and bearings were taken for future reference. We walked back to the carrier. I was never called upon to use a No. 18 set again.

I cannot recall how long I stayed with the carrier. Did I spend the night? However long it was, I was soon relieved and directed back to the battery commander's OP, where he was working in liaison with the battalion commander of 1st Battalion of the Tyneside Scots. The defence of the Rauray spur was soon to begin, as powerful elements of the German Panzers supported by Panzer grenadiers were preparing to launch a heavy attack on the 49th Division positions. I have a recollection of meeting one of my former fellow officer cadets at Ilkley. We came face to face in the bocage close to the enemy. We recognised each other, but made no acknowledgement. He would have been a lieutenant serving in 217 Battery 55th Anti-Tank Regiment, which was in the 49th Division. I was still a gunner, and was not sorry to be in the ranks. I cannot remember his name. I hope he survived the war. Manning anti-tank guns was a dangerous business.

I have another recollection. Maj. Lucas had a despatch rider who would follow behind the major's vehicle and be sent off with a message if radio communication broke down. He was not a pleasant fellow, usually sneering and making sarcastic remarks. No one liked him. He was a loner, and in retrospect I can see he had probably experienced an unhappy childhood and lacked social skills. One day quite early in the campaign he went missing. Had he been killed or taken prisoner? No one had witnessed either of these possibilities. After some time we learned that he had deserted and fled to the beaches, where he was eventually picked up by the military police. We never saw him again, nor did we ever learn his fate. We were astonished at his behaviour, and thought even less of him than we had before.

The first letters home

I must have written one or two letters prior to the earliest one I have saved, dated 9 August. To the best of my memory the earliest letters were subject to censorship by troop officers. I recall writing a letter in which I mentioned Tilly, and I was asked by the GPO if I was giving away location secrets, as our gun position was not far from Tilly-sur-Suelles. I was referring, however, to a Scottish girl Maurice and I had met in London. I must have satisfied the GPO, as I believe the letter was received by my mother. By the time I wrote the first letter that has been preserved, the troops were using Army privilege envelopes (see below). I had to certify on my honour that the contents of the envelope referred to nothing but private and family affairs. Censorship was abandoned. Because of this there are few references to the campaign in any of my letters.

On 1 July the 49th Infantry Division was engaged in an important battle at Rauray. Today you can find a war memorial outside the rebuilt village, listing all the units of the division, to commemorate the part played by 49th Division in the bloody encounter. There is no mention of this fact in any of my letters extant or lost, but on 1 July there was a major assault by two Panzer divisions, the 9th SS Pz (Höhenstaufen) and the 2nd SS Pz (Das Reich), on the front held by the British 49th. It was also my twenty-first birthday on 1 July. I had been with the infantry, the Tyneside Scots,

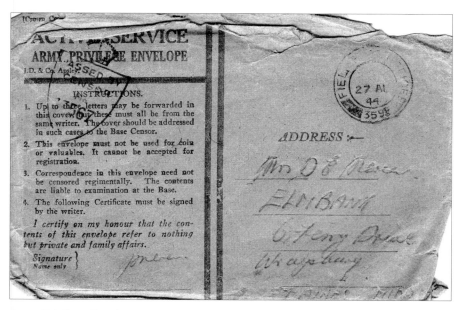

Army Privilege Envelope, 27 August 1944.

the day before, but had been directed to 274 Battery HQ to the rear of the village. I was told to man the field telephone (called a Don R.) linked to the guns. I found shelter in an abandoned German foxhole close to the major's half-track. I was supposed to stay awake all night, but I was tired and fell asleep, oblivious to the telephone signals being sent from the other end of the line. The next thing I knew, a furious line-laying bombardier was cursing me because he had had to trace the line all the way from the gun position to my foxhole. I suppose I could have been court-martialled for falling asleep on duty, but I heard no more of it.

The battle raged all around us that day. Major Lucas, our battery commander, later received the military cross for his masterly targeting of the guns against the Panzers. It was our gunfire that constantly broke up the enemy attack.[11] When the pall of battle lifted, I climbed out of my hole and walked towards Lt Youlton. A mortar shell landed nearby and a splinter neatly removed his nose. I hastened to him and applied my field dressing to his bloody face. Just then Lt-Col. McKay, our regimental commander, came along in his Jeep, and seeing the incident took him away for medical aid. In 1997 I had the pleasure of staying with Lt Youlton's son, a recently retired major, also a gunner, and I took him to meet the men of the 274 Battery Old Comrades Association in Leeds. Unfortunately, this has now been disbanded because there are so few survivors. Our colonel was never far away from the action, and received the DSO for the fine performance of his regiment at this battle. We were sometimes called the long-distance snipers by infantrymen, but without us they could not have won the war. It was the concentration of artillery fire in support of the infantry and tanks that forced back an enemy attack. The Germans wondered if our guns were fired electrically as they switched such concentrated fire as required. In one sense they were, as it was possible to deploy the fire in such heavy numbers when required because of the inter-radio links.

An ordinary soldier sees very little of a battle. His view may be from a ditch and all he can see is a hedge bank. If he is lucky he may have a wider view of a sloping hillside and a group of farm buildings. His war is to keep looking, and firing at what he may see. Often the British and German infantry in the Normandy bocage saw little of each other. The enemy was there somewhere, and a move into the open could attract a burst of machine-gun fire. German mortars killed more of our men than machine-gun or rifle fire. If you were in a tank you had a limited view through a periscope. If the tank commander stood up in the open turret to get a better view, he was likely to be killed by small arms fire. Since it was the British who were attacking most of the time, the Germans had the advantage; they were hidden away in the hedges and embankments, and only opened fire at the last moment. We had the advantage of greater numbers; they had better equipment.

German tanks were better armoured and carried a heavier punch. We met three types of tanks in Normandy. The most numerous were the Mark IVs, which were well armoured and carried a long-barrelled 75 mm gun. There was the Panther, more heavily armoured, also with a 75 mm gun. This was the most popular tank with the tank crews. Then there was the Tiger, a formidable giant with an 88 mm gun, slow but more powerful than any Allied tank. Every British soldier in Normandy heard of the legendary power of the Tiger. Often a Mark IV or a Panther was spotted as a Tiger. The main Allied tank was the Sherman, with a less powerful 75 mm gun than the German. They were manoeuvrable but lacked armour equivalent to that of any German tank. When hit they had a tendency to catch fire. Tank for tank, it was an unequal fight, with the German tank having every advantage of gun and amour. It could take three Shermans to destroy one Tiger. The Germans were confident in their tanks. Our tank crews suffered from inferior models. Only the Firefly, late on the scene, a Sherman with a gun firing a 17 lb armour-piercing shell – imported from a ground-based anti-tank gun – could take on the Tigers and press home a successful attack.

The Germans had a large number of self-propelled armoured guns, called Stürmgeshütze (assault guns). These were to support the infantry in their attack, but increasingly they were used to supplement the German tank units. When it came to artillery, it was the British who had superior weaponry; we were able to switch targets very swiftly. The Germans had nothing like that, but they had the Nebelwerfer, the 'Moaning Minnie', a multi-barrelled mortar that did so much damage.

Letter dated 9 August 1944:
Dear Mother,

Many thanks for the two letters received yesterday & also one from Sibyl. They are dated 3rd, 4th & 5th respectively.

So glad you are with me all along the line regarding faith. There is no need to say more. Yes, I have received parcel containing the paste, ink, cigs etc. & I think I thanked you for it in an earlier letter. Many thanks also for tin of Elastoplast. (Damn these mosquitoes, they are peeling off like dive-bombers & making a thorough nuisance of themselves. I shall be glad when we can get out of this low-lying area into healthier regions.)

I quite understand the fag position & I agree that it is not worth the trouble to send me duty-free cigarettes. In any case I am okay for fags again so you can spend the money on your own smoke-lined lungs!

Thanking you for fags received to date. You see we get a free issue of 50 per week & also we can buy at cheap prices up to 100 per week from the NAAFI. All this should last me, but at the time when I wrote asking for fags the NAAFI had not been around for over a week & I was nearly out. I don't know how I shall get on with pipe tobacco, though. I may have to ask you to get me some. Thank you very much for all you have done. No one could ask for better attention & certainly no one could have a better Mother. Take a neat bow!

So glad that your attitude to horses has changed. I can see you riding with the hounds yet! My pen has just run out of ink & as it is 4 am & I am on duty in the Command Post I shall have to finish *ce lettre* in pencil.[12]

I feel sure that my letters read more cheerfully now. I will tell you why I was so depressed a couple of weeks ago. When we moved into this sector we were told it was a hot one & we soon found out. The German artillery was quite heavy & it had the audacity to answer us back. The whole of the area was under enemy observation & he used to plaster all the roads and villages at will. Our artillery is good (our Div is quite famous now & and is held in respect out here) & so we decided to silence his artillery with our massed fire. Naturally he turned on us & we had some blokes killed. It was a case of who got knocked out first. Well our artillery was far superior in numbers and deployment & after a few days, old Jerry quietened down a lot. He still lobs a few shells over but very discreetly, for he knows that for every shell he fires he will get 10 back. At the same time as these artillery duels the *Luftwaffe* paid us a visit every night without fail & became quite personal. We had a small bomb dropped in the entrance of our dug-out. God be praised it did no harm. At the same time I had raging toothache and ALSO a slight bilious attack!! If ever a man suffered!![13] I seriously doubt and hope that such a combination will ever assail me again, so you will understand why I felt war-weary & now feel my old self again.

I hope I have committed no breach of military security in telling you all this, or caused you unnecessary worry & alarm. Believe me the infantry have it a thousand times worse!

Have you got my pyjamas yet? I sent them back about five days ago in a box.[14] Please tell Sybil that I will write to her soon. Thank her for her nice letter & say that she must be brave (?!) like me & have her tooth out. It really is worth it.

The Allied aircraft have been very active over here lately. I cannot see how the Germans can stand up to us. Although I detest them for being such violent enemies I can't help but admire their courage and tenacity. I don't know how we would face up to massed artillery fire and enormous air

George 'Tiffy' Newson.

Maurice Tyerman.

fleets. George and I have a fit when a couple of *Messerschmitt*s come over! But then our lads had the same trouble at the beginning of the war & the Germans are only having a taste of their own medicine in a stiffer form.

No doubt of it, though, the war is a dreadful thing & to think that human beings have to withstand such a battering makes my blood run cold. And we fire and fire our shells and aircraft bomb, yet when it is all over the Germans who are left alive pop out of their holes & put up a stiff fight. They must be fanatics. If only we could make them understand that we don't want to murder them all, I am sure the German army would surrender en masse. The trouble is they have been brought up to believe that all prisoners we take are killed. What a diabolical system Hitler has imposed on the German nation. What a lot of blood will be needlessly shed before this war is over. However, as the Normans say when you ask them about their ruined homes – *C'est la guerre.*

No more now. All my love to you & convey my love & regards to all at home – Muffets, Syb, Mrs Jones (has she received my letter via Sybil yet?), Godfreys, Boyles etc.[15] Keep faith and *prenez- garde.* John XXXX.

The troop was on the edge of a copse that abutted a series of devastated corn fields. We had moved from the bocage to the rolling plain to the south-east of Caen, over which heavy fighting had taken place prior to Operation Goodwood. As we left our gun position at Audrieu to follow a long and circuitous route a shell landed on our dugout. We had got out just in time. Our first gun position was under enemy observation and counter-battery fire had killed Bdr Dougie Marshall and severely wounded Gnr Johnnie Fever and Dvr Penhaligon. As a consequence the troop was moved to the copse. The nearest destroyed villages were Culverville and Demouville. The ground was easily dug sand. George and I dug deep and had overhead protection from the remains of a ruined cottage. We went over the devastated villages and picked up as much wood as we could carry. A return to Normandy in the 1960s showed new roads and neat suburban houses where the old villages had been. It was ironic that Dougie Marshall had been killed. A few days before, he was heard to remark, 'If ever I get back to Leeds I won't even cross the road without someone holding my hand.'

Camembert cheese and 'nightmare duff'

From the War Diary, 24-29 July:
Counter bty task fired by regt in reply to enemy shelling. General Area DEMOUVILLE again bombed by enemy aircraft. No casualties. Bdr

Marshall D 274 Fd Bty was killed and 1 OR wounded by enemy shell fragments. A tp fd bty was moved to alternative posn during the night.

Although not stated in the diary, there had been a tragic accident involving some of our unit. It had been arranged for members of our regiment to be taken by three-ton trucks to the beaches to give them a rest of a few hours. I went on one of the rest visits. It was very pleasant to sit near the beach, take our shirts off and sunbathe. We looked for somewhere to buy food, but the only café open had Camembert cheese in those round containers we had at home; so we ate our cheese with sticky fingers. Several days later a truck containing a rest group went over a mine and blew up. Our truck had parked in the same field a few days earlier. We had been assured that all the mines had been cleared, but one had not. I cannot recall if any were killed or injured, or from which unit they came.

When positioned near to Demouville and subjected to night bombing and occasional shelling, as previously recorded, we suffered from mosquitoes. These were larger and more virulent that any of us had experienced back home. Some of the lads were badly bitten. We covered our faces with camouflage gauze and were issued with anti-mosquito ointment, which for many seemed to attract the little beasts even more! The soil being sandy, George and I made a deep dugout with an entrance and two adjoining trenches, one for each of us to sleep in. We were proud of our ingenuity and invited others to inspect our handiwork. Once tucked down below we were free from attacks from the insects. While we were in this gun position the cooks brought us some tasty chocolate pudding. George called it 'nightmare duff' because, he said, it made you have nightmares wanting more. The cooks were put out at having their pudding so called until George explained, and then they laughed with all the others and the name 'nightmare duff' spread through the regiment. When I was sitting up in our splendid dugout one evening cleaning my glasses, he said I was cleaning them in order to see my dreams better. George was a wag.

Letter dated 26 August 1944 (This must have been written when we were approaching Pont Audemer, where we were hoping to cross the Seine. The army postal service was so good. In spite of constant moves, our mail arrived, if not on time, eventually. Time is a relative concept in war anyway.):
Dear Mother,

Yea, verily I say unto you a shoal of mail has descended upon me! A total of four letters from you. Just in time as I was beginning to get mighty worried. In a scrappy letter I wrote yesterday I said that I had not heard from you for ages.

It is lovely weather again & I am snatching a few minutes to write, I hope, a reasonably long letter. I will answer your letters in order of age beginning with 20th and ending with 23rd. Glad you are making the best of your job. Being out most of the day is better than being alone in the post.[16] Still, it must be very tiring.

Yes, the war out here is going very well. We are 'swanning' on (an RAF expression that has caught on & is suggestive of a swan flying with its neck stuck out) & I think the next real stand the Germans will make will be on the Maginot or Siegfried lines. Unless Russia breaks into Germany I doubt if the war will end this year, as I should imagine they will be able to hold us at the Siegfried Line during bad weather. But should Russia have new sweeping successes plus our great advances it is likely that something could happen inside Germany. The trouble is that the Nazis are real fanatics & will fight to the last. The high-ups know that Germany is finished but will make their troops fight on hoping to keep Nazidom alive in the spirit of martyrdom for many years. I know that the ordinary German soldier is kept in complete ignorance of what is going on, & according to the BBC even some senior officers are given a false picture to keep them fighting. It is possible that in such a miserable façade something will collapse. It is possible SS troops may end up fighting the *Reichwehr* (ordinary German army not Nazi storm troopers). Anyway, at risk of repetition I will say, hope for the best & prepare for the worst.

So glad that your Anderson shelter has arrived.[17] What a pity you have not got me to put it up. Still, if I were home you would not need it anyway! When it is put up & you have the new lodger, I should most certainly sleep in it, unless you find it too distasteful, both mentally and physically. It will be much nicer for you when she arrives & I hope you get on with her all right. What is her name? You must tell me all about her when you get to know her well.

It was nice for you to have a little do with the 90 year old girl in Garston Lane. Is she really 90 or were you pulling my leg? Also glad to learn that your chase of gentleman Eric is getting along okay. I would like some gory details about *cet homme*.[18] Have you been able to give Sybil my little note? I hope her mother pulls round. Give my deep regards to them both.

A couple of days ago we pulled into a village & found out that we were the first British troops the villagers had seen. The enemy had pulled out a few hours ago. Mr Small & Sgt Gawler deputised for the troop & were given a marvellous ovation. They were taken into each cottage in turn & loaded with cider, milk, eggs & flowers! They came back & dished out their presents accordingly. I had a pint of milk and a new egg!

There is no doubt that the French are delighted to get rid of the Germans (as if the fall of Paris was not enough to show my point). However, the *Maquis* or FFI[19] are really organised & they have been active around us, co-operating with the foot-sloggers. They have a big advantage in knowing the country & correspond to our old LDV.[20] They wear any old clothes & their uniform is an armband with the famous Cross of Lorraine emblazoned on.

As we advance along the lanes the locals throw flowers, cheer like fury & when we stop they zoom up with liquid refreshment. They are very excited & wave and shout & seem quite impervious to any Jerry shells that come back. All my cynicism about the Germans and the French resistance has gone. The proof of the pudding is in the eating! I could tell you some extraordinary stories about the underground movements.

Yes, I have received the 100 Greys & Aspros & also pyjamas plus nougat. Many thanks. No sign of Friday's tobacco consignment but I do not expect that yet. I will write to Chuck[21] when I have time, but it won't be yet awhile. I do hope your toothache & headache have abated now. I am looking forward to seeing you after the war with a nice set of teeth. They must come out you know, but do not worry – I'll hold your hand. I hope the Doodles[22] are better now. I hope you won't be troubled much longer by them, as our troops will soon be nearing their horrible lairs. So bear up, keep faith, give each other courage & behold the sun is shining already! Not a mid-day heat, it is true, but nevertheless an early morning rise with undoubted expectations of a quick ascension. Not a very good parable, I am afraid.

I have not seen Maurice for a long time, but I rang him up a number of days ago, and he was all right. We have not got any time for jaunts these days. Thank you for Cecil's enclosures. I wrote to him a couple of weeks back, so he knows my address. Did I tell you that in a local rag that Mrs Shefferd sent me I saw that Pete Holdstock had been awarded the George Medal? You will remember that he lived in Barnehurst & joined the navy just before the war broke out.[23]

Yes, I liked the apples very much & the pipe is excellent too. Many thanks. We get lots of apples now as there are hundreds of orchards in the country through which we are moving. Yum yum. I am looking forward to the cake. Above all, my dear, keep up your letter writing as I pray nothing so much as a letter from you, and other people, but especially from you.

I hope you can see that picture with Ida Lupino & Paul Hendried in it. It should be good. Won't it be a marvellous thing to be able to go the pictures, as & when we will, when the war is finished. I have been writing this in between targets & while our guns have been pouring shells into the enemy territory. I would love to tell you where I am & where I have been, but that will have to wait.

Well, my dear, this is a lovely letter, long & interesting I hope. Give my love & regards to Muffets, Godfrey, Boyles, cousins etc, and of course, Sybil & her mother if you see them. Take care of yourself. John X.

Towards Le Havre

From the War Diary, 27 August:
Fire plan arranged with 69 Fd Regt grouped under comd 185 Fd Regt. Advance continuing with little opposition towards Pont Audemer. Regt at 15 minutes notice.
Regt Ops carried out registration of prominent pts across river and HF fire[24] onto suitable area behind Pont Audemer.
Regt fired M tgts[25] for Ops or AOP[26] during the evening. Attack by SWB[27] and ESSEX across River Lisle.
Regt fired on DF task[28] as covering fire.
U tgts[29] fired on reports of French partisans.

At this stage of the war the 49th Division was pushing the enemy towards the Seine following the breakout from Caen and the Falaise gap, where many of the enemy had been trapped. It was the beginning of the disintegration of the German Army in Normandy. The Germans were fighting fierce rearguard actions as they retreated, but they were leaving a lot of equipment behind. We came across tins of cooking fat, which we appropriated and used to cook chips (made from potatoes dug from adjacent fields). We had our own cooks, who normally supplied the gun positions with a daily meal. Into our mess tins were slapped hard biscuits, margarine, jam, bacon and a pudding. I remember that the bacon came in tins packed with cellophane and as the bacon was pulled out of the tin the cellophane floated away in the wind to entwine itself in neighbouring trees. Each man had to work out which portion should go where in the two mess tins we carried. The cooks fed us as we queued at the back of the lorry. Our chips were supplementary. When on the move the feeding was much more irregular. Those up at the OP could have no food brought to them by three-tonners. Some came by Jeep, but in the height of battle we relied on two or three days' rations carried by each OP member. When later we shared an OP with some Americans they were glad to swap their pre-packed rations for some of our hot delivered food.

Keeping ourselves clean was a constant concern. We would wash our faces and hands as circumstances would permit and occasionally our feet.

We would shave daily if possible. One had to have water and soap and time. Back at the gun position it was possible to wash our socks and hang them out to dry. Changing a shirt was more of a problem, as the one taken off had to be washed. The thick khaki shirts were not easy to wash and far from easy to dry. I don't think I changed my shirt more than once when in the field, but once we went to the mobile bath unit and obtained a complete change of clothes. When up with the infantry we could not always wash or shave, but if all was quiet this would be possible. No one would attempt ablutions of any kind if it was dangerous. In quiet times the infantry would come out of the line after two days, and we would accompany them in and out, but sometimes infantry had to stay in battle over longer periods until they, and we, would return to the rear, exhausted and hungry, grey-faced with fatigue and dirt, longing to sleep anywhere, anyhow. Just to drop down and sleep, perhaps to be shaken awake after a couple of hours. We were tense but not really alert. I have mentioned before that my chief memory of Normandy was always feeling tired.

The next letter is dated 22 October, but much had happened between the letter above and the next one in October.

The battery crossed the Seine at Rouen. The town had been badly bombed, and driving through the streets filled with debris was a slow task. Often a bulldozer was needed to clear a pathway. Heavy bombing by the RAF to handicap enemy movements also had the effect of handicapping our own advances. All the road bridges were down. At last we reached a railway bridge that had been blown but was capable of taking traffic driven gingerly. It sagged in the middle, and the Seine flowed around the broken railway lines. We got out of our vehicles and walked beside them as each driver slowly proceeded along the perilous pathway. Our Bren carrier and GP trucks got to the other side, and the four quads pulling guns and limbers followed. We had made it. As we drove up the steep hill beyond the bridge we could see other vehicles coming over. Then Lt Cannell, our GP officer, cried out that the bridge had collapsed, and units of the Polish Armoured Division that were following disappeared into the river. (I returned to Rouen in 2008, and found I had just gone over the new railway bridge, arriving by train from Paris. I discovered that it had been blown by the Germans just before we had arrived to cross.) Our cooks were left on the other side and we had to manage with our captured fat and potatoes from the fields for several days until all our units were across by another route.

That night it poured with rain. Three of us were sleeping in a ditch, which soon filled with water. Fortunately we had our waterproof gas capes beneath us, so only our blankets got wet. It took me over a week to get them dried out. It was not a happy night, with little sleep. We drove on to our gun position beside a farm. I had no idea where we were. The War Diary records that it was Rolleville. Usually I was able to work out where we were by looking at the maps that the officers carried. We were somewhere outside Le Havre.

L/Sgt Gawler had a nasty shock as he led his gun crew towards Le Harve. He drove into a group of German soldiers going along a narrow lane towards Le Havre in the same direction. In this advance the guns were sometimes ahead of the infantry. The Germans halted, turned their anti-tank gun around, and prepared to open fire. The British gun crew also halted, and feverishly unlimbered the 25-pounder to face the enemy 100 yards down the road. The Germans got a round off first. It was armour-piercing, and it swished viciously over the heads of the toiling British. Sgt Gawler had to get his squad out of the line of fire before the reply could be fired. The quad driver sweated and strained at the wheel to get the vehicle off the road and out of the way, only too aware that the next enemy shell was likely to tear into the quad. The enemy did not fire again. It was their turn to work desperately at taking their gun out of action, and beat a hasty retreat. By the time the 25-pounder was turned round and ready to fire, the enemy were rounding the bend in the lane. The shell fell into the hedgerow, sending up clods of earth and pieces of vegetation. 'We've got too far ahead,' stated the gun sergeant rather obviously to his surprised and shaken crew. The quad drove around with some difficulty, the gun was limbered up once more, and the unit retreated down the lane until they met another gun crew coming along. They awaited further orders before venturing on towards Le Havre.

Capt. Thomson, who had been wounded while we were in the bocage, now returned, and he asked me to be his OP wireless operator. After several

Fd Mar. Von Runstedt inspecting Le Havre defences, 1944.

The deadly 88 mm gun being moved at Fontaine-le-Malet, September 1944.

days of quiet preparation the assault on Le Havre began. The operation involved two infantry divisions, the 49th and the 51st Highland. These were supported by tank regiments and corps artillery. The codename for the operation was Astonia. It was vital to free the Channel ports, as all supplies were being carried from the Normandy beaches by trucks, and the lines of communication were getting longer.

Le Havre was heavily fortified against attack from the sea. The landward defences were incomplete, but considerable minefields had been laid and a deep anti-tank ditch had been dug. Many concrete pillboxes and underground forts, called bunkers, had been constructed with interlocking fields of fire for anti-tank guns and machine guns. They were supported by field guns and anti-aircraft guns of various calibres. The defence of Le Havre was entrusted to Col. Eberhard Wildermuth. He was not a regular soldier, but had wide experience of battle. He commanded a garrison of some 12,000 men made up from many units. There was a fortress cadre and a security regiment, which had both been defending the port against a long-awaited naval attack, and there were elements of Wehrmacht forces that had retreated into Le Havre and had been hastily organised into defensive companies. As one German officer was to say later, 'We could have held out for weeks had we properly organised and equipped our troops.'

A prisoner of war

There were two heavy air attacks on the defended areas. Large numbers of Lancaster and Halifax bombers caused enormous explosions, creating a huge curtain of smoke and debris. After the second attack our assault began. I did not realise at first what was happening. Tanks and infantry advanced across a vast field. Our carrier was accompanying the Gloucesters with one of the Hobart 'Funnies'[30] on the right flank. The enemy guns began to fire airbursts, and one or two of our infantry, walking widely spaced around us, fell. I was in direct radio contact with Maj. Lucas, our battery commander, and I gave him a running commentary on our progress. As we went forward towards the white tapes indicating a cleared pathway through the enemy minefield, a blanket roll, from a carrier that had received a direct hit from a hidden anti-tank gun, flew through the air and lodged in our left-hand track. Our carrier slewed to the left and stopped. Fortunately we were partly concealed by a Churchill tank firing its machine guns at some enemy hidden by the smoke of battle. Everyone jumped out of the carrier except me; I had to remain on the wireless set. Pulling and pushing, and with the driver, Bdr Smith, engaging the engine carefully to aid the release of the offending blanket roll, did the trick. We were clear, and moved forward over the cleared minefield. It was getting dark by now, and the carrier pulled up in the lee of a high bank with trees giving a canopy above. Exhausted, as much by nervous tension as by tiredness, I dropped into a momentary sleep.

Polar Bear attack on Le Havre, supported by the 'Funnies', flails and scissor-bridge. (*Imperial War Museum BU-859*)

The next thing I knew was a German helmet peering over the side and a cry of 'Hände hoch!' I put my hands up and the German looked inside and disconnected the wireless aerial. 'Raus!'[31] Taken to the other side of the bank, I found Bdr Smith, Pearce, the second signaller, and Capt. Thompson. We were all prisoners. It seemed that Thompson had gone forward on foot to find the company commander of the Gloucesters, and had bumped into a German patrol. He had called out a warning but we had not heard him. (Many years later, I found out when visiting the Gloucesters' Regimental Museum that the company commander, Maj. Lance, had been killed earlier that day.) No sooner were we captured than our own artillery opened up with shells landing a little too close for comfort. British and Germans lay down together until the shellfire lifted. I spoke to the lieutenant in charge, using my halting grammar school German. He was from Hamburg, and was a year younger than me. He asked if we were Canadian. It seems that they hated and feared the Canadian soldiers. I assured him that we were English. As we were led off down a steep hillside, an occasional German would emerge from a foxhole and join us. I began to discard anything that would be of use to enemy intelligence. I threw away the artillery code. I inadvertently threw away some newly minted franc notes that had been issued to us. What else did I have on me? My cigarettes in a flat tin, my emergency chocolate pack, my water bottle attached to my belt, and my plastic identity tags round my neck on a piece of string. No, I would keep all of those. As we reached a pathway we came under fire from some Bofors,[32] which were being used on this occasion to fire tracer shells to indicate the path to be taken in the dark by advancing infantry. We dived to the ground.

Once more on our feet, we were counted. One of us was missing. I learned later that this was Bdr Smith, who made his way back to the abandoned carrier and drove it back to the gun lines. How he found his way in the dark I do not know. He received the Military Medal for this.

I did not think about escaping. It never really occurred to me. My immediate reaction was that I was out of the war. Then I realised that as a POW I would have to be taken to Germany and suffer danger from allied air raids. I next thought that this was nonsense, because how could I be taken to Germany when Le Havre was bound to fall soon? So I concentrated on the here and now. We were led to a huge underground bunker and confronted by an officer, immaculately dressed, wearing Russian front medals and accompanied by his batman, a tall Obergefreite,[33] also with Russian medals. The officer was Hauptman[34] Kurt Langer of the Alpine Corps. He questioned Thomson, who merely gave name rank and number. We did the same. He picked up a field telephone and reported to a superior officer, 'Wir haben ein Funkwagen gefunden.'[35] We were offered food, but taking the cue from our captain, we shook our heads. Several medical officers came in wearing bloodstained aprons. It was apparent that there were wounded people in another part of the bunker.

Thompson was led away by Langer, and Jim Pearce and I were taken to a long corridor and guarded by the tall Obergefreite holding a Luger[36] at the ready. To the side were bunks full of wounded soldiers. The night wore on. We could hear the sound of battle getting nearer. Some French girls came down the corridor and argued with me over the bombing. So many civilians killed, they said. I could only reply, 'C'est la guerre'.

Around 5 a.m. Thomson came down the corridor to tell us that we were no longer prisoners. He had spent the night with his German counterpart, drinking champagne, and had persuaded him that the best course of action was for him to surrender to us for the sake of the wounded in his care. This would be an honourable surrender, he insisted. Langer had agreed and asked that he might go to his billet and get his greatcoat. He reported to his superior officer on the telephone his course of action, and asked those of his men who were still able, to choose between surrender and continuing the fight. My lieutenant from Hamburg and two men volunteered to fight on, and left the bunker. Thomson and Langer left for the greatcoat and Jim and I were left with a dozen or so German soldiers. To our amazement and embarrassment, several crowded around calling us comrade and showing us photographs of their mother, wife or children. 'No more war for me! No Russian front! I go to Canada to POW camp!' they cried. Until now all German soldiers had been grey, hard, dangerous. Now they seemed to be like ourselves, human. We backed away, not knowing how to deal with the situation.

We were saved by the return of the two officers. Thompson told me to lead out of the bunker. I grabbed a Mauser[37] and tied a white tea towel around the muzzle. Then, cautiously, I led the able-bodied Germans out and to the surface. I tried to hand over my former captors to the first infantrymen who came along, but they were in no mood for prisoners. They were skirmishing forward, looking for the enemy. I waited until all were out of the bunker and tried to hand over the captives to the next platoon. To my dismay they stopped to search the prisoners, taking from them watches, rings and anything of value. I told them to stop. We had been treated honourably by these Germans and robbing them like this I found offensive. 'Oh, they'll have everything stripped from them when they get to the prison cage,' said the sergeant. 'We'll just get in first.'

I moved on with my captives through the edge of the ruined village of Fontaine-le-Malet. I had not been more than five minutes along the path when German shellfire burst among us. There was a cry for stretcher-bearers to the right, where some of our advancing infantry had been

Captured German troops. (*Imperial War Museum*, B10170)

shattered by the shelling. I left my prisoners and dashed to give what help I could. When I regained the path (it was the one we had walked down in the dark some twelve hours ago), I found the bodies of Hauptman Langer and his Gefreiter lying dead on the hillside. It seems they had taken up the rear of the prisoners and been caught by their own gunfire. Capt. Thomson, walking between them, had been sheltered from death by the bodies of his two companions. The German captain's smart peaked cap lay beside his body. I hesitated. Should I take it as a souvenir? No, I could not do that. So I left it lying there next to its owner's body. In vain I looked for Thomson and the others. I must have spent longer in the village on my errand of mercy than I had realised. As I walked on down the hill I questioned advancing soldiers that I met. No, we haven't seen any German prisoners, was the repeated reply.

 Eventually I found my way to the gun position, across the battlefield of the previous day, where I was greeted with joy and incredulity. 'We thought you were dead', shouted George. 'We'll fry you some chips!' My mates came up to shake me by the hand and congratulate me on my survival. Later I made my way to the wagon lines to be interrogated. I was so tired. I could barely put a sentence together. I was told to sleep, given a blanket, and I slept for hours.

I have returned to Le Havre twice. Both occasions were organised by a former captain, Ian Hammerton of the 22nd Dragoons, and members of the French resistance. On the second occasion in 2005 my son came with me and we were warmly received in Fontaine-le-Malet and in the town of Le Havre itself. Ian Hammerton was in command of a section of the 'Funnies', and we were close to each other during the assault. Later he and I taught at the same school and it was only after eleven years of sharing the staffroom that we found out that we had been battle comrades. You did not talk about the war much, if at all, in the thirty years following the war. Nearly all the staff at Hurstmere County Secondary School, in Sidcup, had been in the war, but it was not the done thing to talk about it. Only when you are growing older do your thoughts become more public.[38]

After Le Havre the division went on rest in the Bolbec area. I was questioned by war correspondents, who thought I might have a story. I do not know just what happened to me, but I could not talk to them. I was asked my name and address but for the life of me I could not tell them. I suppose it was delayed shock. Today it might be described at battle trauma. They looked at me curiously and moved away to a more forthcoming source. However some version of the adventure got back home as there was a paragraph in the *Evening Standard* saying that Gnr J. Mercer of Wraysbury had been taken prisoner and had then taken his captors prisoner. My mother sent me a cutting. I wrote nothing of this in any of my letters, so seeing that paragraph in the paper must have been a shock to her. I soon recovered my composure and left my trauma behind me. I am sure that talking about the war later in life helped to get rid of any such condition. I was never one to bottle things up.

From the War Diary for Rolleville, 10-11 September:

10	1900	Attack proceeding very well at GLOS front. OP with 2 SWB requests conc DICE and other targets.
	2100	2 ESSEX with 191 bty in sp moving fwd from assembly area.
	2110	274 bty request quick smoke screen to cover adv from en strong point. This could not be produced before darkness.
	2230	Ops report all localities in objectives. 2 GLOS and 2 SWB now held.
11	0200	Capt. Thomson and two sigs captured by the enemy, who later surrendered themselves to their captives when realising they were surrounded.

You may observe that the War Diary puts a slightly different interpretation on the incident.

After the attack on Le Havre, the division went on rest for several days. Our regiment was sited near the small town of Bolbec. I had the opportunity to seek out Maurice. I remember a group of us strolled into town to sample the local wines. We were disappointed. Others had got to the cafés before us and had drunk all of it. We had to make do with crème de menthe. We sipped it and turned away. It was not to our taste. Wandering among the crowd of happy soldiery I noticed what I thought were balloons floating across the evening sky. My companions laughed at me. 'They're not balloons, you chump, they're French letters!' How innocent can you be?

Once rested and cleaned up, we were on the move again. The colonel ordered all his regiment to parade past him as he took the salute. When our Chevrolet command post truck came past him, with Lt Cannell standing in the front, returning the salute, the colonel bellowed at him, 'Get all that gear off the roof! You are a shambles!'

Shamefaced, Cannell stopped the truck. He and his batman clambered over the roof and threw down a large carpet and cooking utensils claimed from the fleeing Germans. Our GPO liked his command post to be as comfortable as possible and had 'liberated' the carpet to put on the floor of his next dugout. But the colonel would not let him have it. 'We don't have all this rubbish in my regiment,' he shouted.

Having lost his precious acquisitions, Cannell resumed his place in the vehicle, saluted, and drove on, muttering. I observed all this from the Bren carrier as I was now Captain Thomson's signaller again.

We clattered through France and into Belgium.

NOTES

1. A Liberty ship was one of many built in the USA shipyards where the hulls were welded rather than fixed with rivets. They were built in record time.
2. OP was an observation post, i.e. a troop commander with his staff of signallers and an assistant forward with the infantry company commander. OP Acks were junior non-commissioned officers skilled in gunnery techniques who worked with the officers in plotting targets.
3. A truck for the use of gun position officers.
4. A Bren carrier was a tracked vehicle.
5. Quads were four-wheel-driven vehicles designed to pull a gun and its limber. They had accommodation for the gun crew.
6. A troop consisted of four guns. I was in 'A' troop. There were two troops to a battery and three batteries in a regiment.
7. George Newson was now a gun artificer. He was known as Tiffy.
8. A concentration of fire.
9. The bocage was a network of small fields and woods encompassed by high

banks. It was difficult to advance through but easy to defend. The German tanks could be hidden hull down behind the banks and camouflaged with greenery.

10. A heavy electrical battery needed to power the wireless sets.

11. See *Breaking the Panzers* by K. Baverstock. Sutton Publishing, 2002.

12. My mother had a fear of horses. As a signaller I would be on duty to receive any fire orders sent from the observation post located with the forward infantry.

13. I had an abscess on a tooth. I reported sick and was taken with others by truck to the nearest first aid post. It was a dangerous drive. The slightest cloud of dust sent up by the truck could result in enemy shelling of the road. Fortunately we were driven with great care. But each trip seemed to last an age. I was seen by a dentist with a white gown over his uniform, and had the offending tooth removed. 'Eeh, if ever a man suffered!' was a catchphrase from the very popular wartime Saturday night radio programme *Happidrome*, with its signature tune 'Ramsbottom and Enoch and Me'. 'Me' was Harry Korris as 'Mr Lovejoy', forever exasperated by the gormless Enoch.

14. I wore pyjama trousers under my battledress to prevent my skin rubbing. I was ribbed at first by the lads but they soon got used to it.

15. Sybil was a lodger in my mother's bungalow. Muffit was my mother's sister-in-law, in whose bungalow we had taken refuge in 1940. Mr Boyle was the Home Guard sergeant who was a professional cartoonist. Mrs Jones I cannot place after all these years.

16. My mother was a full-time air raid warden employed by Staines Urban District Council. There was a wardens' post on the edge of the town with communication to allied services. Presumably this change of duty took her out of the post on a more mobile role.

17. The Anderson shelter was so-called after the Home Secretary, Sir John Anderson. It was made of heavy duty corrugated iron and had to be assembled and placed below ground and covered with sandbags. Wraysbury was late to get them and it was impossible to bury them as the water table was so high. When I came home I put it together with my mother's help and it became a garden shed.

18. Eric was an elderly gentleman living close by with his widowed mother. He had won the Military Medal in the First World War. He and my mother were just friends.

19. The FFI (*Force Française d'Interior*) was a network of resistance fighters loyal to General de Gaulle. There were competing cells and ideas, but all strove to defeat the occupying Germans.

20. Local Defence Volunteers. The original name of the Home Guard.

21. Chuck was an American airman. He was Sybil's lover; I recall that my mother did not like him coming to spend the night with Sybil. My mother did not approve of sex before marriage, but she did not want to lose her lodger nor to upset her, because she liked her.

22. Doodlebugs: Hitler's terror weapon, the V-1. They were launched against London in June 1944 and later against Antwerp when it was captured by the British.

23. Peter Holdstock went to school with me.

24. Harassing fire on predetermined targets.

25. A regimental target, i.e. 24 guns (25 pounders).

26. Air observation post.

27. South Wales Borderers.
28. Defensive fire to aid the infantry.
29. A divisional target, i.e. three regiments of field artillery plus a medium regiment of 5.5-inch guns.
30. Gen. Hobart had set up the 79th Division to be equipped with tanks converted for special duties. Some carried a huge mortar to be used to destroy strong points, others carried bridge building equipment, others were fitted with chains to act as flails to explode mines.
31. 'Get out!'
32. A Bofors was a quick-firing small calibre anti-aircraft gun. On this occasion they were employed to fire tracers on a fixed line to guide the advancing troops.
33. Lance corporal.
34. Captain.
35. 'We have found a radio car.'
36. An automatic pistol much prized by British troops. German small arms were much better designed and manufactured than ours.
37. A German rifle.
38. See *Achtung Minen* by Ian Hammerton. Book Guild, 1991.

CHAPTER THREE

Belgium

We were catching up with our advancing troops, who were pursuing the Germans. When we set off after our first halt for the night, we were joined by infantrymen, who climbed aboard. They were taking advantage of any transport to hasten their way forward. It was exhilarating. We passed through the First World War battlefields so bitterly fought over by our fathers: Poperinghe, Ypres, Passchendaele. We passed war cemeteries. Our fathers had fought the Germans and won, and now we were doing the same.

It was very warm weather and our eyes stung with the wind. The next day we all had eye drops to aid our recovery from exposure to the elements. At one stage I looked up and called attention to the aircraft flying above us. There was wave after wave of aircraft towing gliders, all flying steadily over us and into the distance. Where were they going, we wondered? Later we learned of the attempt to capture the Rhine bridges and the gallant and costly failure to take Arnhem. I had been to school with Ken Washer and I knew he had become a paratrooper. Was he part of that operation? I never found out. The thought often occurs to me that as we moved through our schooling in the 1930s, with intimations of war growing, we did not know what was in store for us. I left school in July 1939: not an auspicious time to begin to earn my living. My parents were both volunteers in the civil defence and not unnaturally I joined in as well and for the first three months of the war I was enrolled as a messenger at the wage of £1 a week, a sum that was repeated when I joined Barclays Bank, Sidcup, in January 1940. A mere pittance.

From the War Diary, 25-26 September:

25   2000   2 SWB[1] occupied posns across the canal. WEST of RE br at 936076 and reported all quiet with patrols forward. DF tasks in sp 2 SWB and also 2 ESSEX who were relieving

KOYLI[2] after midnight, arranged during evening.

26 0330   Attack against 2 SWBs posns developed from NORTH bk of canal. D coy withdrawn slightly.

0400   DF tasks fired against attack until 0415 hrs followed by series of MIKE tgts on suspected enemy FORs.

In my earlier book, *Mike Target*,[3] I copied the pages of a letter that is now missing. It described the above. I added my comments:

I think I may as well describe that incident when our brigade established a bridgehead over a canal. We had moved up quickly and went into action not far from the bank. We were the first troops in the area at the time, the infantry not having arrived yet. I was with the OP and we went to a village nearby for the night and to contact the Recce.[4] Later we found that a big factory about half a mile away from the guns was full of Germans, the only thing between them and the guns being the cookhouse. Incidentally, the White Brigade or Belgian Resistance, magnificently organised, cleared the enemy out of the factory the next day. That day at dusk our infantry with our carrier crossed over the canal and dug in, in a semicircle around the bridge. It was most eerie moving up into the hostile territory at walking speed, wondering what opposition we would meet. I had to have a blanket over my head and over the radio so as to muffle the noise of a chattering radio. We reached our objectives without any opposition and waited for the inevitable counter-attack. Obviously Jerry allowed us to cross the canal, so that he could counter-attack along the bank and cut us off. He nearly did so, too, at one time being only a hundred yards from the bridge.

Anyway, we settled down to uneasy sleep with some infantry in a big barn. At 3 a.m. the Germans started to infiltrate into our positions under cover of darkness. The forward section of our infantry became cut off, and dawn broke to find our position completely surrounded, the nearest enemy being two hundred yards away in a hedge bottom. From three o'clock onwards I was sitting in the carrier outside the barn manning the radio. Our position was under small arms fire, and did those *Spandau* bullets zip and crackle over! It was a good job that the Germans did not have any mortars with them; as it was they did fire some rifle grenades at us. Two exploded in the roof twenty feet from the carrier. I am no hero, but I could not resist peeping over the top of the carrier occasionally to see what was going on. The rest of the carrier crew were in the barn and our officer had to shout messages to me, as he could not reach me on account of enemy fire. The infantry were magnificent. They fired everything they had got, and we saw some of their work later when

German prisoners came in. We had a machine gun, salvaged from a tank, mounted on our carrier, and an infantry bloke was firing this straight ahead until the flaming thing jammed. Our captain decided to call our guns to help and we brought down a troop target on the Germans in the aforesaid hedge bottom. It was what was called a 'close target' because the enemy to be shelled were only two hundred yards away from us. The designation 'close target' meant that each gun layer had to have his work checked by the gun position officer before the order to fire could be given. Our own shells exploded uncomfortably close and it pays tribute to our fire orders and the gunners' accuracy that the rounds dropped fair and square on the target. Of a dozen Germans, all were killed or wounded. Peeping over the side in the other direction I could see bobbing heads and bottoms along a hedgerow some seventy yards away. They were German all right but I never found out where they went. They did not seem to fire at us.

I asked for tanks (code name Big Boys) over the air and these came trundling up about an hour later, by which time the situation was less intense, thanks to our artillery support and the courage of our infantry. I saw a tank go right up to the window of a house about four hundred yards away and open fire through the window with its gun. I pity the Germans inside. Altogether the infantry took seventy prisoners and I saw some horribly wounded casualties. I could not help feeling sorry for them. All the Germans were in bad shape, covered in mud and utterly fagged out.

Reflecting on that letter, now brown with age, I can add one or two details. The German leader of the counter-attack was a middle-aged *Feldwebel*.[5] He wore the white piping of the infantry. I recall that when surrendering he kept looking at his wounded men and sadly shaking his head. The prisoners who were not casualties were ordered to dig graves for their men who had been killed. They were reluctant to do so, fearing that they were digging their own graves. But this was not the intention. After the battle was over and the tanks had rumbled back carrying British and German wounded away, an 88 mm arrived on the scene and proceeded to shell the bridgehead area. The major's half-track was stationed just over the bridge and Bombardier Stead, the major's gunnery assistant, was killed instantly by an exploding shell. I felt cut up about this for a while for although he had never been a friend of mine he was a man I had always liked and respected. It seemed ironic that he should have been killed, and not one of us at the forward OP, where danger had been nearer. When we were relieved by fresh troops we re-crossed the canal and slept soundly after twenty-four hours of fear, sleeplessness and concentration.

The entry in the War Diary is typically concise:

From the War Diary, 26 September:
0000 Considerable shelling and mortaring of bridgehead. One OPA[6]
      killed by enemy action.

A month later, still in Belgium, I wrote another long letter to my mother
that led to some reflections on European politics:

Letter dated 22 October (from which some pages are lost):

Time – 2130

Dear Mother,

I have laid hands on some nice paper and cannot resist taking up pen
and scribing a long letter. I have written every day for almost a week, so
I do not know what I am going to say, but I hope to get inspiration as I
write, my pen permitting.

I had a nice letter from Peter[7] today, in which he told a joke. An evacuee
was sent to the country. The first day he was there he cut his foster-
mother's clothes line & let the clothes fall in the mud. The second day he
did the same, so when her husband came home in the evening, she said

Four gun sergeants of 'A' troop, 274 Battery: Owens, Davis, Roberts and Gawler, in
Belgium, 1944.

she could not put up with the boy, but the old man decided to give him a little longer in which to settle down. The next day the evacuee got hold of the cat and shaved its hair off. Once again her husband persuaded her to give the boy another chance. The following day the evacuee cut off a leg belonging to one of the husband's cockerels. This was the last straw, so the wife sat down and wrote the following letter to the boy's mother. 'Dear Madam, I am sorry but your son will have to return to you. He has let my clothes down twice, shaved my pussy and last night cut a foot off my old man's cock!' A bit near the knuckle, but quite funny!

A short while ago it was suspected that a bunch of Germans were hiding in a wood near our guns. They had been cut off during an advance and had gone to ground. Volunteers were called for from our Battery to mop them up and it was expected that they would be ready to give themselves up. I volunteered (I have a reputation to keep up now) and loaded with weapons including a revolver I set off with the others. We found absolutely nothing & trudged over miles of wood and marshland. It was just as well we did not meet anybody because we were lovely targets. I think most of the blokes imagined they were hauling 25 pounders[8] behind them!

George saw Maurice today laying a line. He is raving about a girl he met in Antwerp, a teacher and student of philosophy.[9] I have not seen him since we met in the baths.[10] Dennis[11] is due off the OP this week. His turn of duty is finished. I am wondering if it will be my turn again. I certainly hope not. It is being arranged that everybody will have 48 hrs leave in Brussels but how soon I do not know. Like many army ideas, it may never materialise.

I think I may as well describe that peculiar noise a *Spandau*[12] makes. A British Bren gun goes 'rat-tat-tat' etc and fires evenly. A *Spandau*, however, sort of pops and snicks and fires at a much higher rate of fire and is irregular. It crackles. It is very peculiar & very unpleasant. I don't think I have given any state secrets away by telling you this. No names of towns or areas, nor units nor formations nor times nor place. I am afraid I am not one of those modest individuals who refuses to talk about his experiences. I like to get them off my chest, & in view of our correspondence regarding this sort of thing, I know you will like to read it.

I hope you, Aunt Daisie & Macbeth[13] are having a nice, quiet time at home now, Sunday evening. I can picture you around the fire, reading, knitting, talking, laughing and listening to the wireless with one ear open. It is warm, cosy and secluded and the familiar furniture radiates the flickering firelight. Outside it may be raining or snowing, but inside the lounge you are undisturbed and self-contained. In the kitchen a kettle is boiling on the stove, and the teacups are set out in clean array for the nightly cup of tea. Who knows? There may be some bread and cheese in the pantry and a bottle of beer brought all the way from Staines on the floor. But, enough! This vision is too good to be true, it is a mirage put before me to tantalise and distract. Never in the history of the world have so many people been made to realise what home is and what it stands for, and what a supreme way of life is peace and concord.

I sometimes wonder if war is worth the terrible cost in human lives and the breaking up of civilised communities. Would it not be better to accept the invader and make the best of things? Had I lived in France would I have been a collaborator? I do not know. Action is governed by impulse, circumstance and to a sensitive man, public opinion. Being sensitive to public opinion and having a conscience I should probably have resisted the Germans, but at the back of my mind I would have had misgivings. The Nazi doctrines are wrong, very wrong, and in the long run I would probably have lost my misgivings. I am sure that that happened in France to a good many people.

The basis, of course, is that war can be avoided. Of that I have no doubt. If nations are honest, and this indicts our own country as well, war can be avoided. After all, war is primarily caused by trade and economic rivalry, this one no less than previous ones, although ideology creeps into the present with probably heavier steps. There is a revolution at the back of this war, pulsating to various degrees, and out of the maelstrom a new conception of society. The age of unrestricted capitalism is over, yet monopolistic capitalism is still strong. If England is not careful we may have a neo-fascist state after the war is over. Does Socialism offer the solution? I think so, but I may be wrong. At least it is worth trying. & no government can make a bigger mess than did the Conservatives before this war.[14]

How can peace in Europe be kept? The solution, as I see it, lies in federation, although this will take many years and have violent opposition. Each country in Europe can be autonomous, but will send representatives to a central government, which will determine foreign and economic affairs. How then can Germany fight France if she is a fellow state? And what will she fight for? Not trade, because that is administered for the benefit of the entire unit. Not domination, because she should not need it with equitable ordering of Europe. If Germany should become aggressive the whole of Europe would be against her from the start and in any case the armies would probably be international. If you doubt the probability of such a federation, remember that England, Ireland, Wales and Scotland were warring factions at one time. All this, of course, after Germany has been suitably dealt with after this war. I am one of the last persons to absolve German responsibility for the crimes she has committed.

All this is a long letter & a high-minded treatise.[15] I hope you have not been bored. Show this to the Muffs and Boyles & ask what they think.

Keep faith, *prenez garde*. Love, John.

P.S. Love and regards to all at home. Hell's teeth, this is some letter.

It would seem that when I wrote the 22 October letter I was unaware of the meeting at 3 p.m. of some of our officers with the Americans:

From the War Diary, 21-24 October:
HECRT 8414

21   During the day there was little enemy activity on 56 bde front. Div concs were, however, repeatedly fired in area of 146 bde who encountered enemy inf and tks NORTH of WUSTWEZEL [*sic*].

22   1100   FOO 191 bty accompanied armd recce from C sqn 9 RTR towards HEESBOSSCHEN. Smoke fired to asst coln to maintain direction.

      1500   CO 2ic and Bcs from 385 US arty bn 104 US inf div visited the regt and arrangements were made for taking over the sector.

A group of greasy gunners. George is on the extreme right. Belgium, 1944.

On the next day I would have been aware of the change as we moved to an area south of Esschen. Looking at the 1:250,000 scale Baedeker map of Belgium and Luxembourg, it would seem that we had crossed the Turnhout Canal in September and taken up positions around Rijkevorsel. I recall an enemy OP in a church steeple, in a village called Hoogstraten, causing our South Wales Borderers some trouble. Our regimental commander came up to review the situation. This was Lt-Col. Mackay-Lewis, known to us as 'Charlie Handlebars' on account of his remarkable moustache. He said to us, the carrier crew, 'Hoogstraten reminds me of the comedian fellow on the wireless, Gillie Potter. He talks about where he lives in Hogsnorton. Let's try a 17 pounder anti-tank gun to knock the top off the tower.'

The anti-tank gun was driven up, and after several abortive attempts, Charlie Handlebars ordered an air strike, so the guns were given a close target and they fired red smoke as the Tempest arrived. This required close liaison between ground troops and the Air Force. It was essential to get the timing right; too soon and the aircraft would just see vestiges of smoke blowing away; too late and the pilot would be gone. He would not be likely to make a second attempt without the smoke to direct him. Our soldiers were close to the target. I transmitted the order to fire. The red smoke arrived all around the target. The Tempest roared out of a low flight path and discharged its two rockets. We crouched down, feeling they were too damned close for our good. The rocket-firing Tempest was an awesome weapon. The rockets hit the tower and the steeple fell to the ground. Our infantry surged forward and chased the enemy out of the village. The enemy OP was destroyed and the village was occupied, and defence against a counter-attack was set up. I recall that the platoon commander was a young Welshman not long overseas. He exhibited enthusiasm and lack of care for his safety that more mature officers had learned to show only with experience. I hope he survived the war, for I never saw him again. Esschen is on the way to Rosendall, so we were on the Belgian-Dutch border. It was low-lying land, quite marshy in places, but there were also a number of pine woods, some extensive.

There was an unpleasant incident as the new gun positions were being decided. An 'O' group (orders group) had been assembled in a farmyard. Officers from the three batteries and the infantry they were supporting gathered around maps. Lt Mitchell came in our carrier. Suddenly there was a burst of fire from an adjacent barn. Several officers were hit by enemy fire directed from a window in the hayloft. Mitchell escaped, luckily. A bullet passed through his steel helmet and knocked it off his head without causing him any injury. Shots were returned to the window, but inside the barn there was a commotion. German soldiers emerged, forcing another in front of them. In a moment all could have been gunned down by our alarmed officers. But one of the Germans cried out not to shoot as they put up their hands to surrender. It seemed that one zealous soldier had opened fire on the 'O' group, but that his comrades had overpowered him and forced him out of the barn. This incident demonstrated the uncertainty of war. You think you are in a safe situation and the unexpected happens. It was my experience that often when you think little is going to happen and all seems calm, that is when something unpleasant and deadly does happen. The opposite of serendipity.

Further action in the Low Countries, and the withdrawal to Roeselare

There is no further letter preserved until 26 March 1945, but much happened in the meantime.

From the War Diary, November 1944:
OUD GASTEL

1   Regt moved to new fwd areas in OUD GASTEL … Some enemy shelling during morning caused three cas to 191 bty, one fatal. Premature reported from B tp at 0930 hrs, gun breech block being severed from breech ring, badly injuring two gun numbers. Believed caused by double shotting.[16]

3   0310 H hr for CROCUS. Village of STAMPERSGAT[17] bombarded for 30 mins previous to 2 GLOS attacking from EAST. Opposition was hy, especially from dug-in tk in village. Concs of fire repeatedly called for before daylight.

Our gun position was in the village of Oud Gastel. The ground was soggy and it was not possible to make a decent dugout. Sometimes we were offered a bed in a farmhouse, but when this did occur we usually refused, feeling too dirty to sleep in a real bed. I seem to remember we slept in the hay above the cows. It was customary for farmers in this area to have the cowshed attached to the farmhouse. You opened a door from the living room into the cowshed. The cows were kept very clean but the cowshed smelt strongly of cows and their droppings. Some of the lads could not stomach the smell and found an alternative place to sleep, under or inside a vehicle. I put up with the cows as the shed was waterproof and the cows warmed us, and we were lulled to sleep by the munching as they chewed the cud. It was now November, with winter chill on the increase. I seem to remember that Capt. Thomson had his eye on one of the pretty village girls. She wore bright red shoes and lifted the hearts of all who saw her.

When we were back in Normandy in the Demouville area, we had been visited by an Army padre. He had dropped down into the dugout that George and I shared and asked if we would like to be confirmed. Neither of us had been brought up to go to church. My late father did not believe in churchgoing, but he would never be hostile to the church, respecting it as a stabilising institution. George and I looked at each other. We had said some prayers at times of danger. We both knew the Lord's Prayer by heart; if it was not taught at home by parents or grandparents, it would be taught at school. Today children are not taught the Lord's Prayer at school. A sad situation, I think. We agreed to be confirmed, and the padre promised to return and give us some instruction.

He did return, but not to give us instruction. He came to the gun position to say that a confirmation service would be conducted at Eindhoven in a few days' time: 'I'm sorry I have not been able to give you any instruction at all, but I've had other things to do, and it's been quite impossible to keep track of all the units since the break out. But you'll be all right, won't you?'

We mumbled that we supposed we would be. We agreed to go – as much as to get away from the front as to receive holy blessing. A three-tonner turned up in due course and several of our troop climbed aboard. The service was held in the works theatre of Philips, the maker of electrical goods. Altogether there must have been nearly 100 men assembled. Officers and men, mostly in war-stained battledress and muddy boots, from many units of the division, sat in the auditorium seats. The Bishop of Dover arrived and conducted the confirmation service. To my surprise I saw Gnr Medhurst going forward. He knelt before the bishop ahead of me. He was the last person I expected to see there. He was a gun number in 'A' troop, a big, tough-looking guy with a crew cut; but I recall he was a gentle person, and I had never seen him in any kind of scrape. George and I came away from the service somewhat awed and subdued, not quite sure what we had done or what had been done to us.

Many years later I learned about the stressful duties expected of a padre in the field. He had to identify the dead and bury them, to comfort the dying, to console the wounded and the nerve-shattered, and to write condolence letters. It was particularly stressful to get body pieces out of a crippled tank, and even worse if the tank had gone up in flames, burning and charring the occupants.

We returned to Oud Gastel. I have a photograph of Wally Coldrick and me standing in a garden with some Dutch boys playing. I remember being concerned about them lest they got into any kind of danger. There were cartridge cases lying about and guns with ammunition. Suppose the enemy opened fire upon the gun position and killed some of the children? Years

Wally Coldrick and the author at Oud Gastel, on the Belgian/Dutch frontier, 1944.

later Rein Hack (see note 17), who was born in Oud Gastel, gave me a current newspaper with the same picture of Wally Coldrick and me. It is reproduced here. I am on the right. Was he one of the boys I was concerned about?

There was quite a lot of enemy activity. The infantry supported by our guns made minor attacks to clear villages, and received counterattacks in return. For some of the division, there were short-leave passes to Brussels.

By this time I was no longer a member of the carrier crew, and was with the guns. Soldiers liked their tea hot and sweet. The cooks' wagon would deliver a great can of tea, and we would queue to have our mugs filled, but the cooks' wagon did not always arrive, as I have indicated earlier, and in any case a small brew-up was always welcome. At the gun position there was usually fuel to boil water, the fuel being unused cartridge bags. Each shell case contained three bags, a red one, a blue one, and a white one. They contained nitro-glycerine, which when ignited in a confined space, such as a gun barrel, caused a violent explosion to propel the shell. However, if ignited in the open, in a small open hole, it would burn with a fierce flame. Often only two of the bags would be required for a particular target; for a distant target, all of the bags; for a closer target, one or two bags. There were always expendable cartridge bags lying about around the guns. During a big barrage many bags would be left unused. It was easy, therefore, to dig a little hole, empty the contents of a discarded bag into it, set the contents alight, and boil water for the tea. It was a privilege enjoyed only by gunners.

In the autumn of 1944 the Allied advance had penetrated into Holland, but the supply chain still stretched from the Normandy landing beaches. Thanks to Mulberry Harbour, vast quantities of food, ammunition and fuel could be landed, weather permitting; but the lines of communication got longer. It was essential to free the Channel ports, but so much damage had been done to them by air bombardment and land attack that none was yet operating effectively. The prize of Antwerp had been hoped for. The port facilities there would have rendered the long and tedious drives from Normandy to the front unnecessary. Unfortunately Antwerp had been rendered virtually unusable on account of minefields in the Schelde estuary and the enemy gun concentrations on Walcheren Island facing the port on the east coast. Therefore the amount of shells was limited, and to cover a long front along the Dutch-Belgian border, the division was reduced in effectiveness and split up into smaller semi-independent brigades. Had the airborne attack on Arnhem been successful and the bridge over the Lower Rhine secured, the war might have been over by Christmas. But it was not to be. The Germans flooded much of Holland, and nearly all forward movement came to an end.

We moved towards Weert and again were confronted by flooded land. We made a night occupation as it was known that the enemy was not far away. As we drove into a farm the quads left the guns and went off to laager. It was necessary to set up a night picket for the gun layers to lay their gun sights on an aiming point. I volunteered to climb onto the top of a hen house to fix the red lamp on which the guns could lay their dial sight. I had no sooner scrambled onto the top and placed the battery light into position than a fusillade of shells descended on our position. I came down much more quickly than I had gone up, and clung to Mother Earth, expecting the next explosion to be my last. However, after another explosion on the other side of the field, there came a number of dull thuds as shells hit the earth but failed to explode. It was obvious that some unknown slave workers had sabotaged the shell fillings or rendered the fuses useless. It seemed to be just one enemy gun that was firing, probably a self-propelled 75 mm. The enemy gunners had got our range accurately enough, but their capacity to do damage was limited. Our guns put down some defensive fire to where the OP thought the 75 mm was, though we never knew how successful we were; but we were not shelled again.

We understood that our brigade was to advance as far as possible to Venlo, a strategic town over the river Maas and on the German border, but this was not to be. One day, as George was planning an even more ambitious dugout, a buzz went round the gun position. 'Tedder's boys are up,' remarked Jim, observing the fighter-bombers of the tactical Air Force going over us to strafe the enemy lines.

'Yes, Jim, Winter Campaign,' someone replied.

'Have you heard the latest?' said another signaller, hot-foot from the command post where Lt Cannell was supervising his latest improvement in protection after several weeks of unsatisfactory cow byres and outhouses. 'We're coming out on rest!'

'On rest?' said one of us. 'Where?'

It turned out we were to be completely withdrawn from the line and returned to Belgium. Our destination was Roeselare, not far from the French border. We drove off in convoy, glad to be away from the mud and the wet and the dangers. We slept under our vehicles just as we had done on our first night ashore in Normandy. As then, there was anti-aircraft fire as shells were fired into the star-filled sky, but this time they were bursting around V-1 flying bombs passing overhead. I remember still the clarity of the stars in the sky. There was no cloud, and every conceivable galaxy was visible. Were V-1s destined for England or Antwerp? As the British had advanced eastwards a number of V-1 and V-2 rocket sites had been overrun, but there were still some left that could bring death and destruction to London or Antwerp. It was one of our aims to clear out all the V-1 and V-2 sites as we advanced.

We halted for the night at a place called Erps-Kwerps, just east of Brussels. What a strange name, I thought. By this time I was feeling ill. I had a fever and stomach pains. I emptied my bowels whenever we stopped. The most convenient place was outside someone's woodshed in the middle of the night, with the crack of shell bursts overhead. Erps-Kwerps seemed a fitting name.

We reached Roeselare early in the morning and stood by our vehicles. An advance party had worked out our civilian billets for everyone. I was sent to a cottage in a row in the centre of the town. It was occupied by two elderly Flemings, Pauline and Joseph Breskels. I was shown into a white-painted, simply furnished room with a feather bed and clean white sheets and woollen blankets. I washed as best I could and climbed into bed. The chamber pot remained a very real necessity.

The following morning I went to the window and looked out. Men of our battery were moving about below, ready to have roll call. 'Bill, tell the sergeant-major that I'm not well and I intend to stay in bed here at no. 46 for a couple of days until I'm fit again,' I said. In normal military circumstances this message on my part would have been unthinkable, but such was the trust and comradeship that had been built up in the troop during the campaign that my unorthodox communication was accepted.

A few minutes later the sergeant-major came to the foot of the cottage. 'Mercer, you should report sick, but just this once you can stay where you are. I'll come and see how you are tomorrow.'

After twenty-four hours I had slept and sweated my fever away. Whether I had just caught a chill or a minor form of dysentery I shall never know. What was remarkable was that I had been living rough and kept well through five months of heat, rain, frost and wind, and in the open most of the time. The idea of living rough today fills me with alarm, but I was young then. I was lucky not to have had even a cold in the head until this time, when I could go to a real bed and sweat myself better in nature's own way. Old Pauline and her husband looked after me like a son. They emptied my pot and brought me warm soup and brandy. They were most appreciative of the Army rations that we brought them. Of all the items they liked, the best was soap.

'You do not smell like German soldiers,' said Pauline.

'How did they smell?'

'It is not easy to say. But their soap was not good. We had to use it. There was no other. It was ersatz.'

It was a smell that we were to meet again and again when occupying quarters that the enemy had just vacated, and that we were to smell in German civilian houses, too.

The Belgians had plenty of potatoes and a little pork. I was amazed at the tasty meals that Pauline could produce with potatoes and vinegar and a little margarine or oil. One day Joseph said that there was a local smallholder who wanted to entertain some English soldiers to thank them for freeing his country from the occupying Germans. George, Dennis and I got ready, and in the early afternoon the man arrived with his donkey cart. We clambered aboard and set off out of town along a poplar-lined road until we turned down a narrow track leading to his smallholding. We were bidden to enter his home and were introduced to his wife and children. We gave them gifts of chocolate and soap. A meal of pork and potatoes were ready for us. It was clear that the pig had been specially slaughtered for the occasion. We smiled and nodded and drank several toasts. We caught the eye of old Joseph and he smiled back and winked. The farmer and his family were not very clean and the farmhouse smelt of pigs and dirty washing and unwashed human beings. I had a job to eat up the generous helping of fatty pork, and had to smile and say how good it was out of politeness. Further offerings were made but we had to refuse. We felt awkward and were glad when we were able to make our excuses and leave. The farmer was clearly disappointed that we were not able to eat any more and to drink a second bottle of brandy. We said to Joseph that we felt embarrassed by our behaviour to our host, but the smell of the place was overpowering. Joseph nodded and smiled. Our combined French was not good. He was a Flemish speaker with a good deal more French than I had, so conversation was difficult. Smiles, winks, nods and gestures were an essential means of communicating. The farmer had been kind to Joseph and his wife during the occupation, giving them black market food. He was a rough man but had a heart of gold. The invitation was his way of thanking us for the liberation of Belgium. When I returned home upon my release I corresponded with Joseph and Pauline every Christmas for a number of years, thanking them for their kindness to me.

Disbanding

Soon, rumours circulated that the regiment was to be disbanded. The gun numbers and many drivers were to be transferred to the infantry. It seems that the infantry had suffered such heavy casualties in Normandy that their numbers had to be supplemented. Manpower at home could not maintain sufficient recruitment. This was a terrible rumour. Many of 274 Battery had been together since 1939. They had been comrades in Iceland, in Wales, in Scotland and in England, and their recent experiences in battle had forged a common bond. That this bond should be broken was unthinkable. To send the gunners into the infantry was a fearful prospect. It was not long before the rumours proved to be true.

From the War Diary, 1-10 December:

1   Preparation to move to YPRES area. CRA 49 Div[18] talked to all
       ranks on the disbandment of the regiment.
3   Move to rest area completed. Troops in Beveren.[19]
7   Address by MGRA to all ranks, especially to those liable for
       retraining as infantry.
10   197 ORs posted to X(iv) List as infantry trainees and taken on
       strength.

I only recall our regimental commander Lt-Col. Mackay-Lewis (i.e. Charlie Handlebars) addressing us. He spoke with some emotion. He told us that he had appealed in the strongest manner not to disband the regiment, but to no avail. He praised us for our courage and duty and said that the DSO he had been awarded was due to the actions of his men. We all felt for him and for ourselves, too. He was promoted to be CRA 43 (W) Division on 11 December. He later became a major-general. When he died in the 1990s I attended his funeral with a few of the old regiment and met his family. He was buried in Layer Marney Church in Essex.

In addition to this honour, during the campaign the following decorations were won by the regiment:

Maj. F. R. Lucas RA	MC
L/Bdr W. Smith	MM
Bdr H. Norgate	MM
Gnr D. E. Gill	MM

The total casualties were:

Killed:	1 officer; 19 ORs
Wounded:	10 officers; 70 ORs

You can imagine the sadness and foreboding with which those drafted into the infantry left us. George kept in touch with one of them, Smudger Smith, a Londoner. He survived the war. I do not know what became of the other 196. Signallers and other tradesmen were posted to various other units. Dennis Bould, George and I were sent to Borg Leopold, a former Belgian Army depot to the east of Brussels. Maurice was sent to an artillery unit of the 52nd Lowland Division fighting on Walcheren Island.

We spent Christmas 1944 in the camp. I arrived with my Mauser rifle and was given a telling-off by some corporal for bearing enemy arms. I tried to explain the circumstances, but he refused to listen. I was marched off to be issued with a .303 service rifle. On Christmas Eve we had passes to go into Brussels. Four of us wandered from café to café, from time to time meeting up with others we knew. There was a good deal of enforced jollity. Many civilians abroad in the streets wished us 'Happy Christmas'. Overhead, all night long, the V-1s rumbled and rattled their way to London. I did not drink enough to get drunk, merely to get sleepy. Some of the lads may have gone looking for women, but we did not. Around three o'clock in the morning I persuaded George to call it a day, and we picked up a military vehicle that took us back to the camp. We turned in for a few hours sleep. Christmas Day was miserable. At 9 a.m. we were awoken by the officers and warrant officers bringing round tea and rum. This is an old British Army tradition. This was followed by Christmas dinner, served also by officers. This cheered us up a little, but the traditional fare and the incongruous surroundings coupled with the after-effects of the drink the night before had a depressing effect on me. The barrack room had one low-powered lamp and it was cold. Snow had already fallen, and much more was to come. Overall the day was not one of celebration. I lay on my bunk, trying to keep warm, and thought of happy Christmases of the past, as a child with my mother and father, and latterly with only my mother.

These thoughts were mingled with forebodings as to the future. Where would I be sent? Would I go with George or with Dennis, or on my own? I fretted over the loss of the regiment and the loss of comradeship built up in the heat of battle. I lay on my hard mattress and fell into troubled sleep.

On Boxing Day morning George was ecstatic. 'There is a symphony concert in Brussels this afternoon in the Palais des Beaux Arts. I've got two tickets. Dennis doesn't want to come, but you'll come with me, won't you?'

I said that I would. I had never listened to classical music before, but was willing to learn.

'They're playing Dvorak's Ninth Symphony, 'The New World'. I've got it at home and play it on my gramophone. I know you'll like it.'

We got a day pass, hurried through our dinner, and took the tram to Brussels. It was a longer journey than we expected and we rushed to the concert hall in an agitated state. The first bars of the national anthems were being played as we entered, ascended the stairs and looked for our seats. Every eye was upon us. Two dishevelled British Tommies in none-too-smart uniforms. The audience on this Boxing Day afternoon was the bourgeoisie of Brussels, men in black ties, women in elegant gowns. We sat red-faced and conspicuous. This was my first experience of concert-going and I sat enrapt, listening to the magical music and watching the players weaving the spell. I have much to thank George for.

On New Year's Day Dennis and I were posted to the 7th Armoured Division Counter Mortar Officer's Staff in Sittard, over the River Maas. This move coincided with a fierce attack by the Luftwaffe on aerodromes used by the Allied air forces. Because of the snow our aircraft were grounded and the aerodromes were taken by surprise. Many aircraft were destroyed on the ground. This was the Luftwaffe's last major action of the war: Operation Hermann. Twenty-seven airbases were hit and put out of action from Brussels to Einhoven. Some 300 Allied aeroplanes were knocked out. The 47th Panzer Corps had begun to advance from the Eifel mountains to cross the River Our as early as 16 December. What became known as the Battle of the Bulge had begun: a desperate attempt to plunge into Belgium, separate the British and American armies, and drive to the Belgian coast. Rumours of this attack had reached Brussels while George, Dennis and I were in Bourg-Léopold, and as we were driven towards Sittard on 1 January there were signs of panic among the Belgian civilians. Some were packing their bags and heading towards the coast. Sittard and its area were not to become a target for the enemy attack. That came further south and was primarily directed against American troops, although British forces were also to be involved.

NOTES

1. 2nd Battalion South Wales Borderers.
2. King's Own Yorkshire Light Infantry.
3. Book Guild, 1990.
4. Reconnaissance; either a forward party of the infantry or a unit of the Reconnaissance Regiment.
5. Sergeant-major.
6. The OPA was Bdr Stead.
7. Peter Reynolds, the son of my mother's best friend (Auntie Maude to me). He was not in the armed forces due to poor health. He wished it were otherwise.
8. The regiment was equipped with guns firing 25 lb shells.
9. Maurice Tyerman had trained as a schoolteacher before called to the Army. He had a considerable influence on me, leading to my later taking up teaching and leaving the bank.
10. At some point in the campaign in Belgium the regiment went, battery by battery, to a mobile bath unit for a very necessary wash and change of clothes. This was when George and I saw Maurice in his birthday suit and pulled his leg about his sex appeal.
11. Dennis Bould was the lance bombardier who had me regraded as a driver/ operator. He and George were my closest friends. When I attended my first reunion in Leeds we did not recognise each other. We had not met for forty-seven years. He was a tailors' cutter and had gone back to his old job when he was released early in 1946.
12. German belt-fed machine gun. The German infantry had far more machine guns in each unit than had the British Army. The Spandau was greatly respected.
13. Auntie Daisy was my late father's eldest sister. She came to stay with my mother from time to time. She had lost her husband in 1940 in the same week that my father was killed, but her husband, Uncle Walter, a sheep farmer on the Isle of Sheppey, was killed accidentally on a practice bomb range. He had been recruited secretly as an underground agent, to become active should the enemy have invaded. Auntie Daisy did not learn of this until after the war. Macbeth must have been one of my mother's cats. I don't remember him.
14. I was an avid reader of *Guilty Men* by Michael Foot, which was a polemic against the prewar Government. I also read *Tribune*, a left-wing periodical.
15. At least I was aware of my political limitations! I was also much taken with the programme put forward for postwar planning by the short-lived Commonwealth Party, which was a strong advocate of a United Europe.
16. This was a sad accident. It was not often a 25 pounder had a breech explosion. It was known to happen more often to the 5 in medium gun.
17. When I was attending a Probus meeting in Sidcup a few years ago I met a Dutchman, Rein Hack, who had married an English girl. He had lived in Stampersgat and was eleven years old at the time of the shelling, and told me ruefully that I had tried to kill him; but he bore no malice. 'Yes,' he said, 'I recall the polar bear on the uniforms. So you were one of them!'
18. CRA was Commander Royal Artillery. He was at divisional headquarters.
19. Beveren was adjacent to Roesalare.

CHAPTER FOUR

Holland

Sittard, Limburg, is an industrial centre in the Dutch coalfield. The province is unlike most of Holland, since it has hills and thick woods. We were billeted in a coal miner's house. It was comfortable and clean. We noted here and elsewhere that the housing stock was better than much to be found back home in England, with central heating, pipes within the house so that the occupants did not freeze, and beautiful paved or wooden floors. Soon we were sent to the pithead baths for showering. These showers were for the miners, and how good they were! I felt really clean for the first time since leaving England. Some of our lads had been miners in the Yorkshire coalfields, and compared their conditions unfavourably with those enjoyed by the Dutch miners. George had been sent elsewhere, but with the same division, the famous 'Desert Rats'. As he was a gun fitter he was posted to the 5th Regiment of the Royal Horse Artillery. Since it was an armoured division, the guns were self-propelled, although the calibre of the guns remained the same. I was not to see George again until after the war. We had a little time on our hands.

The CMOS was still being set up. We all had to learn our duties. Essentially we were to spot enemy mortar sites and inform the guns, so that they could bring down fire before the mortars could move again. In Normandy enemy mortars, especially Nebelwerfers,[1] caused so many casualties that it was decided to set up a special counter mortar unit in every division. The duty was simple. There were two forward outposts well separated from each other. When a mortar was heard to fire, each observer took a compass bearing and immediately the signaller reported to the command post in the rear. From the command post the information of intersection was plotted and the guns given directions for firing. I was attached to Sgt Lloyd's listening post. Dennis went to the command post at the headquarters of the brigade. Our commanding officer was Maj. Crane, and his assistant was Lt Hopper.

Before we moved in the line we saw a film starring Rita Hayworth. She was a favourite pin-up girl with the forces. This was the third film I had seen while campaigning. On one occasion, I cannot recall when or where, a mobile film unit arrived and we were able to sit on the grass and watch a screen in daylight. What the film was I cannot remember, but I was surprised at the time to think how much was done to keep up morale. My late brother-in-law, Jimmy, who had an infantry role with the Royal Engineers in Italy, had a tale to tell about a mobile film unit sent to bolster morale before an assault on Monte Casino. He waited for the film to start. What was it to be? Bing Crosby in his latest? Olivier in *Henry V*? Crackle, crackle, flicker, flicker, went the film. Then up came the title, accompanied by martial music: '*They Died with Their Boots On*, starring Errol Flynn and Olivia de Havilland'. What a morale booster. There was a lot of shouting, and boots were thrown at the screen.

In the Belgian country town of Turnhout, not long before the crossing of the canal described earlier, a cinema had been opened for the troops

They Died with Their Boots On, a 1941 western shown to the Royal Engineers before the asault on Monte Casino.

of 49th Division. George and I went to Turnhout from our encampment, on a steam tram. The cinema was filled with khaki-clad figures and with smoke from a hundred cigarettes. 'This will be good,' said George, 'It's Bing Crosby in *Going My Way*. It's his latest film, about a Roman Catholic priest.' Bing Crosby was a favourite of both of us. The film flickered through the pall of smoke. It opened with the credits, then stopped. It began to flicker again, and one minute into the film it stopped. There was a roar of disapproval from the audience. Then it started and stopped again, the musical accompaniment weirdly distorted. George leaped to his feet. 'Come on Johann. We can't stand this. Let's get out'. So in a fury George left the cinema followed by yours truly. At least the Rita Hayworth film was not spoiled or interrupted.

While in Sittard we also had an ENSA² show. We were very well entertained by a sergeant with a gramophone and records. He made us all laugh with his mimicry and his voice. He had gap teeth. It was none other than Terry-Thomas, who became a successful film and television actor. Then he was an unknown entertainer, a mere sergeant.

According to the War Diary, we had a strength of thirty-five officers and men; a small unit. I was in Sgt Lloyd's listening post, with Bdr Donaldson, three gunners and two other driver/operators. We had an armour-plated half-track to travel in. This vehicle proved invaluable in icy weather. Our first OP was in a convent in the village of Holtum. We used an apple store under the roof to keep watch for mortars. The smell of the apples packed in boxes in paper was pleasant. We had a large skylight to observe through. Before us were fields with the odd tree standing out against a vista of snow and ice. Fortunately we were soon supplied with newly designed tank suits, which were warm and heavy, being lined with kapok and made out of some kind of light canvas. They had elasticated wrists and ankles to keep out the cold. We felt privileged to have them, as we were not tank crews. They made the cold nights on watch more bearable.

The good nuns left us alone. They were, however, discreetly sympathetic. It seems they had hidden Dutchmen on the run and escaped Allied airmen during the occupation, using many subterfuges. We had a room below the apple store where we slept, and one of our gunners was the cook as we had no cook's wagon coming up to us so near to the enemy. He would fetch our rations from somewhere in the rear, and we did well under the arrangement.

It was while we were at Holtum that the full force of the German offensive through the Ardennes took place. Many units of the British Army were diverted to aid the Americans, who were suffering the brunt of the attack, but our division was unaffected and continued to hold the position opposite the Roer River. Night after night I would stare from the skylight across the frozen waste and listen for sounds of the enemy. They were rare. The action was elsewhere. However, I did hear night after night the sound of a motorcycle, the rumble of a tank, the noise of vehicles being driven. These sounds followed a regular pattern and were repeated at regular intervals. I reported that I suspected an amplified recording was being transmitted across the battle zone in order to give us a false impression of enemy activity. This report was subsequently confirmed.

The frost turned to fog. Dense swirls of cold fog came across from the direction of Susteren just within the Dutch border. Often we heard our bombers flying over to bomb targets in Germany. Monchen Gladbach was the town most probably their target. We peered into the fog, half expecting enemy tanks, followed by Panzer grenadiers,[3] to emerge before us. Then the division went on to the offensive on 13 January. It was designated Operation Blackcock. It was strange to listen to the artillery bombardment and see the barrage light up the sky when we ourselves were not responsible for transmitting the fire orders. No longer were we bringing down 'M' targets. Those of us in the CMOS as signallers felt left out of it.

We did not have long to wait. We left Holtum by night and travelled along the single road to Susteren. With the fog had come a temporary thaw. There was mud everywhere. The damp cold penetrated our tank suits. Progress was slow. The enemy was putting up a stiff resistance. As well as the 'pop-pop-brurp' of the Spandaus[4] and the rattle of the Brens there was the crump of enemy shellfire unpleasantly close, and the occasional burst of a mortar bomb. We would soon be in business after all.

We came to a bridge over a narrow river, the Vloed Beek, on the edge of the town. The scene was illuminated by blazing houses and barns. On the bridge itself a field ambulance had been hit by shellfire and was ablaze. Figures ran to and fro, trying to move the ambulance over the bridge and to put out the flames. Nothing could get over the bridge until the vehicle had been moved. Infantry of the 1/5th Queen's worked along the bank of the river, slipping and sliding in the mud, to storm a machine-gun post. It was a scene reminiscent of Dante's *Inferno*; all fire and smoke and cries of pain and anger. After what seemed like an hour, during which time some of us in the half-track got out and helped to push the ambulance over the bridge and out of harm's way, the bridge was clear and the fire extinguished. In fact only a few minutes had elapsed. Many years later I was to discover that a future brother-in-law, John Regan, was one of the ambulance crew. He had been with the 7th Armoured Division in Africa and in Italy, and had experienced much longer military service than I had.

The rest of our night was spent in the cellar of a house in the main street. It had been occupied by the enemy, and only abandoned within the hour. The cellar was still warm from human occupation and smelt of that ersatz soap that Pauline had spoken about. There was no worry about lice or typhus.[5] We were only too glad to lie down on the mattresses and get some rest. I tried to contact the command post on the radio set. All through the night I kept trying to get through, but I had no luck, so I stayed on listening watch, to the accompaniment of a German voice calling, 'Marco, Marco.' Whoever it was, he had the same difficulty with reception as I had had.[6] His melancholy, high-pitched voice went on and on: 'Marco, Marco.' I never knew whether he ever made the contact he was trying to reach, but he effectively stopped me from communicating with our other units. His persistent, ghostly voice sounded forlorn and desperate.

Susteren was cleared by the Queen's, and our listening post was established in a farm looking across moorland towards the village of Montfort. There was no call for mortar sitings, and soon we moved into the village itself. Our half-track entered Montfort at dusk just behind the infantry. There had been a skirmish around the village street and a German soldier lay dead in the middle of the road, his body still warm. I saw he was wearing a belt. I was aware of the uniform leather belt with metal clasp proclaiming the words 'Gott Mit Uns'. Suddenly I wanted that belt.

I said to Les, the driver, 'Help me to turn him over so I can take the belt off him'. One of my companions said, 'How can you do that to a dead body? Leave him alone. He's some mother's son.' But I was determined to claim that belt. I was not to be put off. 'He's dead. He doesn't want that belt any more. I do. I won't be doing him any harm. The harm has been done to him already.' Les helped me to lift the body and I removed the belt and held it up in triumph. It was a good one, newly issued. I put it round my waist and it fitted exactly. I do not record this now with any pleasure. I look back and know I should not have done it. The dead German was probably my age. He was blond. He would have been either in 176 or 183 Infantry Division, or a member of the Parachute Regiment transferred from defending the River Maas to the north. I cannot remember what happened to that belt. I suspect it was abandoned when I was transferred to the 3rd Regiment Royal Horse Artillery in the autumn of 1945; I might have thrown it away in an act of remorse.

Our final stop in this sector was at Posterholst to the east of Montfort and right on the edge of the River Roer, which marked the boundary between Holland and Germany. There were some relatively undamaged houses, quite new, a contrast to the older buildings seen so far. They were on a small housing estate built for prosperous Dutchmen. The houses were empty. Eagerly we took possession, for the weather was extremely cold again. It was a winter of extreme cold throughout northern Europe. We had petrol-burning stoves for our cooking, which was done in the open in case of fire. Bill Mountford, our cook, got cracking, and we had a large container full of hot tea. So cold was the temperature that by the time all the lads had got their mugs from the half-track, the tea was lukewarm, cold in ten minutes and frozen in fifteen. We were amazed at how cold it must have been.

There was a lull in the fighting. Operation Blackcock was over; we had squeezed the enemy out of the Roer pocket and reached the German border all along the river. Soldiers on both sides were able to find accommodation in empty houses and barns and so mitigate the cold.

While we were in Posterholst news came that from now on other ranks could wear collars and ties, and also shoes. Hitherto only officers wore collars and ties as part of their uniform. We had long envied the Americans of all ranks, who had this privilege, as well as remarking on their superior cut and cloth. Dennis was a tailor's cutter in Leeds, so he set about altering shirts. He took cuffs to make collars and strips of shirting to make ties. We all carried needle and thread and spare buttons in our packs. Our so-called 'housewife' (pronounced 'hussif') made a tie for me and converted one of my shirts so that it had a collar. He did the same for himself, and offered to do the same for anyone in the listening posts. He was kept busy for two days, sitting cross-legged on the floor of the house, busily cutting and sewing. Most of the lads were delighted to donate a spare shirt for the enterprise, and were pleased that our little unit was able to outsmart many of the others, who would have to wait for an official issue. Shoes were another matter. These could not be manufactured like the collars and ties. We knew that we would have to wait until we should come across some shoes in an abandoned house somewhere. That would not be looting, we told ourselves. We would not lightly do such a thing in Holland, but once inside Germany we considered shoes fair game. We thought of all the looting the Nazis had done in Europe; this would be giving them a taste of their own medicine.

March was occupied with preparing the assault across the Rhine, which is over a mile wide. This was to be a miniature Normandy landing. I was fortunate to be granted ten days leave in England.

From the War Diary, 1-24 March:

1   In rest billets with HQRA 7 Div HQ at STRAMPROY (5990).

6   Gnr Mercer on leave to UK.

7   Moved to HEEZE.

13   Major Crane, Lt. Hopper and 4 Ors on 48 hrs leave to BRUSSELLS.

18   Lt Hopper & 5 ORs moved to EPPEINGHOVEN (152368) as advance party and functioned as skeleton CM staff from 23rd for RHINE crossings.

19   Gnr Kyte admitted to hospital.
20   Gnr Coldrick on leave to UK.

You will see that I went on leave on 6 March. I travelled by train, passing through flooded polder land. The train must have gone through Utrecht and close to Amsterdam and Rotterdam. The land had not long been cleared of Germans. The train was slow, full of soldiers going on leave. As we came near to Rotterdam we saw crowds of Dutch people, mostly women and children, close to the railway line. They were begging for food. To my horror a line of Dutch police mounted on horses swept towards the crowd with their sabres drawn, to drive then away from the train. They struck some of the people with the flat of the sword, dispersing them; but not before some of the soldiers on the train, myself included, had thrown some of their rations into their midst. We did not realise yet how badly the Dutch had suffered under the Germans (the Dutch name for them was 'Moffer') in the last days of the war. So much of their land was underwater, and they had been deprived of food and accommodation; the older Dutch have not yet forgotten their ordeal under the Germans. This was in contrast to Belgium, where on the whole there was little suffering. It seems that the RAF dropped food by parachute over Holland only where the population was thickest – where it was believed the people were the most in need.

Eventually I got to Calais. I don't recall how long I spent on the train. I must have spent at least thirty-six hours in all, perhaps more. In Calais I embarked on a cross-Channel ferry at dusk, to arrive in Dover early in the morning. I saw many ships sunk in the harbour. The ferry carefully slid alongside a quay, and we were on home soil. I am still amazed at the organisation of the Army to furnish me with the right papers, to plan the journey, to get me on and off ships and get me home and then back again. Where would my unit be on my return? It would be found for me. The British were able to give their troops home leave while the war was on. This was privilege denied to Americans and Canadians. They were too far from home to have such schemes. I have no recollection of the return journey on 16 March, but I learned that one of the ferries had been blown up by a mine during a crossing, and that clearing Calais and Dover completely would take many months.

Returning to the War Diary, you will notice that a number of the CMOS went on leave at this time. Wally Coldrick went on leave to the UK and the two officers went on leave to Brussels.

This letter must have been written at Heeze, soon after my return to Holland:

CMOS group. George Laidlaw is top row left, Sergeant Dyer is top row right. Germany, 1945.

Letter dated 26 March 1945:

Dear Mother,

A few lines in haste. Please forgive the rough paper.

Many thanks for the two letters, two bundles of magazines & papers & my clean clothes parcel. All arrived sometime today. I also had a letter from Mary, the post office wench.[7]

The time is 6pm. & I am sitting in the back of the half-track, which is parked & camouflaged in the middle of a large field. Oh, what fun! No, you need not have worried. I was nowhere near the Guards when they attacked the remaining Germans west of the Rhine.[8] I think in fact, I was home with you at the time!

So pleased that Aunt Maude is going to spend a weekend with you. It will be nice for both of you. The weather has been a bit patchy for the last two days, showers & sunshine mixed. We slept in a tent last night, but were warm & quite comfortable.

I also received a letter from Valerie, which I am enclosing for your perusal. I hope you can decypher it. Ask Hilda[9] to thank her for it & I am replying as soon as possible.

I am pleased that you are going to get advice about your income tax. Mr Boutcher[10] or a consultant will do, as long as you can make it snappy!

It does not matter at all about the collars. I don't suppose I shall need them yet awhile & so unless you have already done so, please do not send them to me until I ask for them. I thank you.

I hope you can do a little in the garden, but do not try if you feel tired. Well, I reckon that is about all for now. I will write again as soon as I can. *Prenez-garde*. Love and regards to Hilda and all others at home. Don't worry & keep well.

John.

It seems that the Division was at rest after Operation Blackcock. The diary records that we were at rest in billets with HQRA & Div HQ at Stramproy. That is a village not far from Weerte, where I had been the previous year with 274 Battery. On my return, the unit had moved to Heeze, a larger village south of Eindhoven. At both places we were well back from the fighting.

NOTES

1. A multi-barrelled mortar that made an unforgettable series of whooshing sounds when fired.
2. Entertainments National Service Association.
3. German infantry trained to work with tanks.

4. A fast-firing belt-operated machine gun.

5. Because there had been an outbreak of typhus in Naples in 1943 during the Italian Campaign, it was deemed advisable to prepare for lice and typhus when fighting in Normandy. As a consequence, every troop had to have one or two men trained to deal with lice should they be encountered. I had volunteered to go on a week's course held at Barton Turf in Norfolk. We stayed in a mansion once owned by Sir Robert Peel, near Barton Broad. We learned about the habits of lice and how to eradicate them with powder. In fact, no British troops became lousy, but some Germans soldiers were lousy when captured.

6. Transmitting by radio could be hazardous. Radio waves would not carry in thick woods, nor close to tall buildings. The weather affected the quality of transmission. Sometimes wavelengths were so close together that the one interfered with the other. A harmonic was when you picked up messages intended for another station. I once heard on my radio net an agitated call from a tank crew to another engaging a Tiger tank in the Normandy bocage.

7. Mary worked on the counter of the post office in Ashford. I used to chat with her when going there on bank business. I think she was more interested in me than I was in her. We never met after the war.

8. This was the bloody attack through the Reichwald Forest to reach the Rhine. This attracted all the available German reserves of infantry, parachutists and armour, and was carried out through country that was favourable to the defender. It was a country of few, indifferent roads, of sodden fields and heavily mined forests. The bulk of the army was British, but it was under the command of the Canadian First Army.

9. Hilda was the lodger, a GPO telephonist, unmarried and in her fifties.

10. Mr Boutcher was the manager of Barclays Bank in Ashford, where I had been a junior clerk.

CHAPTER FIVE

In Germany

From the War Diary, 26-31 March:
HEEZE

26   Main body moved with Div HQ to harbour area at 019252.

27   Joined by adv party after crossing the Rhine.

29   Moved to harbour area 375588 (SW of BORKEN).

According to *A Short History 7th Armoured Division: June 1943-July 1945*, the division crossed the Rhine at two places on 27 March following the assault by the 52nd, 15th Scottish and 53rd Welsh Divisions with the 4th Armoured Brigade. It seems that CMOS crossed at Wesel and moved to a harbour area near Borken. As a counter mortar unit, we were now largely redundant, as the battlefront was constantly moving and we had no sooner set up a listening post than the battle had moved on. The German forces were being split by advancing tanks and infantry, and shelled and bombed. There was breakdown in their lines of communication, loss of supplies, and fragmented command. There was organised resistance where determined officers gathered scattered men together, but there were also desertions. Some soldiers took to the woods and took off their uniforms and dressed in civilian clothes. Others surrendered; but in spite of the chronic collapse of the German Army (and not only in this battle area) there was some organised resistance, and there would be stiff fighting still to come where. We moved with HQRA from now on and were virtually bystanders. Had there been German mortars firing long enough for us to set up listening posts, we would have deployed, but there was another role for us to play, as will be revealed.

By late March, I was feeling optimistic about the impending resolution of the war:

Letter dated Wednesday 28 March:
Dear Mother,

Well, I have not very much news for you. News that would not offend the censor, I mean. I am well apart from a slight cold which I cannot imagine how I have contracted. The weather is cloudy & a little colder, but no rain to speak of.

It is almost like the early days in Normandy again for us, what with sleeping in tents and operating from vehicles etc. Of course, I cannot tell you where I am or what I am doing, except to say that I am writing this in the back of the half-track & everything is quite quiet. The old Jerry planes have been wandering over at night & making a nuisance of themselves, but only on a very small scale. As I have said before it recalls the early Normandy days to my mind.

The war against Germany seems to be going very well as a whole. I do not know how the Red Army is doing but I know that the Yanks & ourselves are doing very well. The war may be over sooner than we expected. Or rather should I say as I expected! I have not heard from you for a couple of days but I expect mail from both of us will be haywire for a time.

This really is a very difficult letter to write as I do not know what to tell you. Still, I expect you can guess a good deal. I can relieve your mind, I think, by saying I am not in the front line. And I guess that is about all! Unsatisfactory isn't it?

I hope you have a pleasant Easter. It will be nice for you to have a little time off from that nasty Squad work.[1] Thanks very much for the clean washing and chocolate parcel, which I received two days ago.

Mary's (the post office girl) was a quaint little affair which deserves a similar answer I suppose. That is when I find myself able to write it. I saw the tail end of George yesterday as he passed by on a motor bike. Just my luck! But I saw some of the other lads who used to be with us & went to RHA with George.

I hope that you are well. Keep faith & do not worry. It looks as if all our blokes will have finished leave by August, so I may be home again in September. That is if they keep the present system going.

No more for now. Love and regards to all at home. I should be able to bring John[2] home my pack filled with loot next time! Take care. John.

The dating of this letter poses a problem. According to the War Diary the unit left Heeze on 26 March. The unit crossed the Rhine on 27 March. I remember seeing a number of crashed gliders at Hamminkeln, where we harboured, some ten miles further into Germany. Writing that the situation reminded me of our early days in Normandy can only refer to our time after having crossed the Rhine. The disparity can only be explained by assuming either the letter was begun on the 26 March and finished later, or that I had got the dates wrong in the first place. Presumably it was written at the harbouring near Borken.

No more letters have been preserved, but once the war was over in May 1945, the need for sending mail in the special green envelopes would have been unnecessary. I do not know exactly when open letters could be written, but it would not have been long after the war's end.

One of the highlights of entering Germany was finding the POW camp at Fallingbostel. It had housed 10,000 British and American prisoners, and doubtless I would have been one of them had the Le Havre capture turned out to the Germans' advantage. When our unit reached the camp it had already been opened up by the 11th Hussars. The German guards had melted away. Men of the 1st Airborne Division were guarding the gate, dressed in scrubbed belts and gaiters and well-creased battledress. How did they do it? They had been prisoners themselves. The camp was being run by RSM Lord of the Airborne. When the German guards had fled, he had taken over and set up a remarkable discipline. Many of the inmates were half-starved and some needed medical attention, but that was not our job. We waved and moved on, exhilarated by the vision of their freeing.

The division was held up a number of times by strong resistance, but by 2 April we had advanced 120 miles into Germany. Each crossroads was dangerous. There would be a hidden anti-tank gun to knock out the leading tank, or a foot soldier with a hidden bazooka, or a cleverly hidden 75 mm mobile gun. Many years after the war, when driving along an English road towards crossroads, I would half anticipate a hidden enemy position about to open fire. That memory has now faded, but traces of war memories sometimes float into one's consciousness. I see a field of waving corn and can visualise German soldiers advancing through it. I see a wooded hillside and imagine our shells exploding into it, creating fearful damage, with splintered branches lacerating the enemy beneath. I see a good spot for an anti-tank gun hidden from the advancing enemy tanks. I recall the white-faced and exhausted enemy prisoners at the Turnhout Canal.

One evening when we were far into Germany and putting up a tent, a solitary German aircraft repeatedly flew over. There were few enemy aircraft to be seen at this stage of the war. The RAF had dominion in the skies, but as the British Army advanced, they closed on the airfields that were still operational, and at dusk or at night the few German aircraft remaining would come over and be a nuisance. I remember on this occasion an intense fear. This lone enemy: was it looking for me? Memories of the Battle of Britain came back to me, of the bomb that had killed my father.

We were both in a public shelter eating the dinner that my mother had left for us in the oven. 'Hitler isn't going to stop me enjoying my dinner,' he had said to me. He was dead five minutes later.

The bomber flying slowly over our unit as we camped for the night brought that horror back to me. I felt scared. Maybe a person only has a finite stock of endurance, and after times of fear and exhaustion, that stock begins to run out. Was my stock coming to an end? The bomber flew away and I gave a sigh of relief. It had not come for me.

As a prison guard

As our unit was moving forward, a staff car overtook us. An officer jumped out and told Sgt Lloyd that we had a new assignment. We were to set up a temporary POW camp. We were conducted to a farm with a large empty field beside it. Within half an hour, the first German soldiers began to arrive unescorted along the road and out of the woods. Most had been in hiding, not knowing what to do or how to give themselves up. Being law-abiding and obedient by upbringing, the Germans knew they had to surrender to the victorious invaders; moreover it was safer to be under the protection of the British, lest they were attacked by marauding Russians freed from a nearby prison camp. Within an hour there were thirty Germans of all shapes and sizes. There was a tall, immaculate Obergefreite of the Luftwaffe in what seemed to be a brand new uniform, his bright yellow lapel markings standing out against the blue of his jacket. There was a young poorly-clad Wehrmacht private, with worn boots, a hat too big for him and a pallid, drawn face; he did not look a day over fourteen. There was a lieutenant with red artillery markings. A middle-aged captain with the white infantry piping became their natural commander. The officers were resigned and cooperative. Indeed, all the prisoners were cooperative, even the Luftwaffe corporal, stiff-necked, arrogant and a pain in the butt to those guarding him. If he did not attempt to run away, he moved and reacted to orders given him by his British captors with slow disdain: what we would call dumb insolence. It is still a matter of regret fifty years later that one of us did not give him a hard shove with the butt of a rifle.

Sgt Lloyd and his men were bemused by this sudden and unexpected change of role. How could we guard these men without a perimeter fence? How could we feed them without extra rations? How could we supply them with bedding, or find water for drinking and washing? Then there would be the problem of latrines.

The guarding became easier when a supply truck drove up from nowhere and dumped some reels of barbed wire on the road. We paid out the wire, tearing our hands on the vicious barbs. We needed heavy duty gloves for this work. As if by magic the truck ceased to vanish into the distance and backed down the road to where we were standing examining our hands. 'Here you are mate,' called the driver, 'You'll need these. I almost forgot them.' We were tossed two pairs of thick, stiff gloves. With these we able to make a boundary fence around the field and farmhouse, hooking the wire onto posts and looping it around the twisted iron supports supplied to hold up the wire. We had just enough for a single strand at waist height to complete the boundary. It would not keep in anyone who wanted to leave. But who would want to do that?

Our thirty prisoners were joined by more than a hundred more in the course of the day. Sgt Lloyd became increasingly worried. 'We can't take any more, boy,' he confided to me. Sometimes he seemed to treat me like a son or a younger brother. 'What can we do if we get any more? I know they are all surrendering, but there's only six of us and we couldn't hold them if they made a charge at us.'

His fears were increased when a further bunch of soldiers plodded in. 'Where on earth are they all coming from?' It was clear that our troops on the advance had been given orders to point in our direction any German soldiers who were surrendering.

Sgt Lloyd's anxiety was partly met by some new arrivals. Six or seven men smartly dressed in brown and white uniforms marched into the farmyard, and their leader saluted. 'We are officers and men of the King of Yugoslavia,' he uttered in perfect English. In bewilderment Sgt Lloyd returned the salute and walked away. What else could happen? Who else might arrive? A squad from the Waffen SS?

There was a sudden diversion as the farm owner, an elderly woman who could have been taken for a witch in a fairytale by the Grimm Brothers, went over to the hand pump in the corner of the yard and found it to be broken. There had been some water for the prisoners, but not any longer. 'Pump kaput!' she screamed, 'Englishen Schweinhunden!' The tired captain went over to her to calm her. He told her it was no good complaining. The pump had not been broken on purpose. She continued to mouth her fury and made her way back to the house shaking her fist as she went. The prisoners looked on in dumb silence. They looked like a herd of cowed and weary cattle.

We talked with the Yugoslavs. Their senior officer was an amazing man, able to speak seven different languages fluently. We did not succeed in finding out just what they were doing in Germany. It seemed that they had been prisoners of some kind. They had belonged to the Royal Army, led by Gen. Michaelovitch, who had first fought the Germans and then Marshal Tito and his communist partisans. In this confusion, the British Government had switched sides and supported Tito, because the communists were more effective in fighting the Germans. Looking back now, those men who had joined us in the farmyard may have been members of the Fascist Croatian Army, which had collaborated with the Germans. Of all these political niceties we knew very little. We welcomed these Yugoslavs as being on our side. We enrolled them into our guard duty and lent them rifles when it was their turn to keep an eye on the prisoners.

The prisoners did not like this arrangement at all. They conferred in groups until finally the captain come over to the sergeant. 'Sergeant, we do not like that we are guarded by these men. We do not recognise them as soldiers. We feel insulted that you have given them guns to guard us. I wish to make the strongest protest.'

Sgt Lloyd drew himself up to his full height of five feet three inches and looked up into the captain's face. 'We need them. You will have to put up with them. You are in no position to make a complaint.'

The captain returned to his men standing in the damp farmyard as the mists of evening began to gather. He explained the situation and shrugged his shoulders. There was nothing to be done. The Germans scowled, but could do little else. They had decided the war was over for them, and that they would have to put up with all manner of things they would find unpleasant. The prisoners were told, using the Yugoslav officer as an interpreter, to pull straw from the barns to make the field less wet to stand in. At the same time they were encouraged to bed down in the straw left in the barns. As night fell, the smell of unwashed bodies, slightly alleviated by that strange smell of the ersatz soap and talcum, indicated the presence of German military.

Two Yugoslavs appeared with a pig, which they intended to slaughter for their evening meal. After some discussion, the would-be butchers were accompanied by Les and me to the farm kitchen, and the witch was summoned. She certainly had spirit. She refused to open the door until we threatened to shoot out the lock. We burst into her kitchen and helped ourselves to two large knives. She must have feared for her life, but we only intended them for use on the pig.

The pig was hung up by its back legs and its throat cut. Its squeals could be heard for miles. Eventually the squeals died away and the pig was emptied of blood. Once this gruesome task was over, which appeared to affect the Yugoslavs not in the least, the animal was cut up into large chunks for cooking on a campfire in the yard. Our barn was almost set on fire, so large was it, and so fiercely did it burn. We were invited to partake of the meal, and some of us did, although at least two of our six declined, being sickened by the butchery. There was nothing for the prisoners except water, which had been fetched from the nearest village house now that the farm pump was broken.

At midday on the morrow, three large trucks arrived with a British interpreter. It was not before time, since the sanitary arrangements were nonexistent for the numbers we had to look after. The prisoners were paraded. They stood in line, weary, hungry and defeated. Even the Luftwaffe corporal looked downcast. The interpreter called them to attention and addressed them briefly. One by one they were ordered on to the waiting vehicles. The old witch appeared, and demanded compensations for the damage to her property, and loss of her pig. 'Yes, yes,' said the interpreter in her own language, 'You may or may not get compensation. You must claim from the military government once the war is over.'

The trucks drove away for the prisoners to be identified, listed, numbered, fed and housed. They were no longer our problem. Our holding operation was over. We received orders to rejoin the CRA. Only the Yugoslavs were left. 'Please do not leave us here,' said their articulate officer. 'We have no arms and we will be attacked by the locals once you are gone. You know we are hated for helping you guard the Germans. News will get around and we shall be killed.' The sergeant was in a dilemma. He scratched his head. He said he was sorry, but he could not do anything more than to take them a mile or two away from the village for their safety, and then leave them to fend for themselves.

This was agreed and so we shook hands all round and Les drove them away as suggested, leaving them a mile or so down the road the way they had come. I still wonder what became of them. They would not be welcomed back to Yugoslavia now that it was controlled by Marshal Tito. If they returned they would stand trial for having belonged to the wrong side, and would probably be executed. Later I was to meet more Yugoslavs before I left the Army for good.

From Bremen to Hamburg

Advancing once more with the rest of the division (we had had been out of the race forward for a day and a half), we clattered along country roads and through more woodlands and heathlands interspersed with smallholdings. The countryside was swarming with green-clad Russians, who had escaped from their prison camps. They were hungry, vengeful and desperate. They would have to be rounded up, brought under control, and sent back to their own country, but that was not our job. We had to press on with the division towards Bremen.

We halted on the outskirts of Bremen; German resistance was hardening once more. There were three incidents worth recording. We met a group of Polish farm workers who were now freed from forced labour. Someone

CMOS group in Germany 1945. The author is first on the left.

produced a camera and several pictures were taken. It seemed from the photograph that I was badly in need of a haircut. The Poles were delighted to be free again, and we were happy in being instrumental in freeing them. I do not recall seeing any farm owners. I suppose they took refuge in their large farmhouses, or had gone with the German forces into Bremen. Civilians were keen to keep out of the way of the invaders. They were in danger of being caught up in a pitched battle, of being attacked by roaming Russian former prisoners, or being set upon by their former slave workers. On the whole they secretly welcomed the British, as they brought with them an assumed sense of fair play, and therefore the likelihood of some order in security: if not immediately, then at least in the long run. The Germans were taught from youth to respect order and authority and they expected that from the British. We had been warned of fanatical resistance to be offered by the underground movement. We were told that there might be secret armies of so-called 'werewolves', who would carry out sabotage and assassinations once we had occupied the country. We expected the same sort of resistance that had been offered by resistance movements in France and Belgium and Holland; but this proved to be a nonexistent threat. There were members of the Volkssturm, a German version of our Home Guard, but many of them had fought with the Wehrmacht, and surrendered with them.

As we were talking with the Polish workers in the April sunshine, and congratulating ourselves on the imminent ending of the war, there was the sound of anti-aircraft fire suddenly bursting overhead. What on earth was going on? We soon found out. A large three-engined Junkers 52 transport plane, the sort made with corrugated aluminium, flew ponderously over the trees ahead of us, trying to gain height. Shells were bursting all around it, and rifle and machine-gun fire joined in the onslaught. It skimmed the treetops, making a great din, pursued by the gunfire. Where it was going, and whether it got there, we never knew. The roar and throb of its engines died away and the firing ceased.

The division was diverted away from Bremen, which was heavily defended. It fell to the 43rd Wessex and 51st Highland Divisions to reduce the city. We came to a small town (was it Hoya or Rethem?). It seemed to be quite deserted, and a tank battle was in progress. We stopped and awaited fresh orders. All this time Sgt Lloyd and his men travelled alone in the half-track. We rarely saw members of the other listening post, or the command post staff. There was a newly built house at the side of the road. It was empty. The door was not locked, so four of us walked in. There was no damage; no one had tried to turn the place over. Perhaps the occupants had left within the hour. Perhaps they were hiding nearby in the woods. It was interesting to see the inside of a prosperous German house. In the living room was a pianola. I had never seen one before. The electricity was still working. Clearly the owners had not been gone long. Someone who had seen a pianola before switched the power on and the piano roll began to play mechanically, filling the room with the strains of a Beethoven sonata. We were surprised and delighted with this new experience. The pianola played on until the end of the roll. Someone looked out of the window to see if we were moving off. The half-track was still there, with Sgt Lloyd looking anxiously at the house. 'Don't worry, Sarge,' we called, 'We'll come as soon as you give the signal.'

The bookcase had a good collection of books. 'Hey, look at what I've found,' I called, 'It's a copy of *Mein Kampf*.' I pulled the book out and opened the front cover. It had been awarded to a resident of the house. It was signed by Hitler. I opened a drawer. Lying in it was a red Nazi armband, with a swastika in black on a white background. Both the book and the armband were legitimate souvenirs. The householders were active party members. No wonder they had made a quick exit. Was there anything else we might take? 'Shoes,' went up the cry. We raced upstairs and looked under the beds and in the wardrobes for the shoes we had promised ourselves. I was lucky. I found a pair of good brown shoes that fitted me pretty well. Some of the others were less fortunate.

An early edition of *Mein Kampf*.

'Get on board!' called Sgt Lloyd. 'We're moving forward.' We left the house as quickly as we could. The wardrobe doors were left open, but nothing else was touched. Even the electric piano was switched off. Anyone returning would have found little changed, and only a book, an armband and three pairs of shoes were missing. We were not being careful for the sake of the residents, whom we believed to be 'bad' Germans, but in case we were caught in the house by some of our own people and accused of looting, which was strictly forbidden, and punishable. Later we were to see signs of wholesale damage and looting, but none of us was ever guilty of that.

It is difficult to convey the chaos in which Germany was now enveloped. Not only was there fierce fighting in pockets and sudden swoops forward where the enemy had withdrawn, but the countryside was on the move. German soldiers were giving themselves up in great numbers, Slave workers were taking to the roads, some walking south, some walking north, some walking in circles, confused as where they might go to get home. There was a breakdown of central and local government, leading to food shortages, news blackouts, rumour upon rumour, and people turning to crime to survive. The German Army was disorganised, with lines of communication lost.

The next day there was fighting in Soltau. As there was no concentration of mortars for us to observe, we had to wait at the rear. As we drove to find a suitable place to spend the night, we were stopped by military police.

'Halt! You can't come down this road. It's out of bounds.'

Mystified, we halted and turned off the road into a clearing in the woods. What was going on? Why was the road out of bounds? Always the curious one, I asked a Redcap who was diverting the traffic what all the fuss was about.

'Can't tell you exactly. It's a health hazard.'
What was a health hazard? This tidbit of information was merely tantalising. I had to know more. After a while some members of the Pioneer Corps came past, looking down and drawn. 'What's going on here? Have you been involved in this health problem that's stopped us going along this road?'

'Yeah, and it's a bleeding awful business,' was the first reply. 'They've found hundred of bodies of slave workers in the woods. They had been allowed to die. All skinny and bags of bone they were. They were buried in shallow graves. The locals have been made to dig them up and give them a proper burial.'

A more eloquent private filled me in with more information. 'We've had to strip all our clothes off and be fumigated in case we carry any infection with us. And there's still more to be buried tomorrow.' Was this the notorious concentration camp at Belsen? Or was it some other horror camp? We never found out, as we were on the move again.

On our advance to Hamburg we passed along an Autobahn that ran through heathland and small woods of pine trees. Several attacks were made on the moving columns by German fighter jets. These were a new phenomenon: jet-driven planes. The Germans had beaten us to it in this area. Our jets were successfully airborne just after the war. Had German jet production got off the ground a year or two earlier, things might have gone rather differently. I took several photographs from a handy ditch of one strafing raid. But from where did I get a camera? The photographs when developed were blurred and useless. On each side of the Autobahn and deep into the heath were large enemy dumps of ammunition and petroleum. Care was needed driving off the road for fear of mines. We came to an abandoned air base and gingerly explored some of the huts for souvenirs. The equipment was superb. Every weapon, every tool, every piece of motor transport was excellently made and extremely functional. We and the Americans outclassed the Germans in sheer volume, but their technology was usually better than ours. Only in artillery and radar equipment were the Allies superior. This may seem a very sweeping statement, and may not have been true of the Air Force and the Navy, but the impression we got in Europe was that the German Army was very well equipped and efficient, and that we had needed our superior numbers to overcome them. Thank God for the superior numbers.

I mentioned earlier that our little unit was to have two unusual roles to play. One was to set up the temporary POW cage of which I have already written. The other was to take over and guard Hamburg Airport. The war was about to end. Negotiations for the surrender of Hamburg had been completed.

NOTES

1. I have no idea what 'Squad work' was.
2. John Barnes was Muffet's son. He got a place in Christ's College in Horsham at about this time.

CHAPTER SIX

Ceasefire and After

From the War Diary, 1-11 May 1945:
Steinbeck

1	0001	Location – Div Det HQRA south of HARBURG (401290). Little activity.
4	1440	Move to new ALG on HAMBURG airport 65046203.
5	0755	Two FWs 190 land on airstrip – had flown from OSLO – pilots taken to Div HQ for interrogation. Hostilities in NW Europe ceased.
6		Move to new ALG at 140097 (near ITZEHOE).
9		Gnr Kerridge returns ex UK leave. Gnr Wanbon leaves for UK.
10		Move to new ALG at 006197 (NORTH of KIEL Canal).

On 29 April a deputation approached our lines, consisting of two staff officers and a civilian. They had come to explore the possibility of securing immunity from artillery fire for the hospital at Harburg. This developed into negotiations for the surrender of the city. Letters were exchanged between Maj.-Gen. Lynne, the Divisional Commander, and Maj.-Gen. Wolz, Commander of the Hamburg garrison. It was agreed that all officials would remain at their posts until replaced. There would be no demolitions. All SS troops had already marched away. On 3 May, the division moved over the River Elbe to occupy Hamburg. No difficulties were incurred, other than the embarrassment of many German staff officers, who eagerly awaited orders in the town commandants' office. Eventually a galaxy of splendidly dressed German officers emerged.

Our two half-tracks were ordered to enter the airport and ensure that
no acts of sabotage took place. Somewhat overwhelmed by our orders, we
drove up to the gates. They were opened by airport police, who were armed
with neat Luger pistols. They saluted smartly and let us through. The police
were dressed in light green uniforms with strange leather helmets rather
like those once worn by our postmen. They were asked to hand over their
weapons, which they did, somewhat reluctantly. The next day a staff officer
drove up and demanded that the police should be given back their pistols.
It seems that Lynne had agreed that the police would be allowed to keep
their small arms, otherwise they, the police, could not guarantee order in the
city; so the two sergeants of our unit had to be found and told to return the
pistols they had taken. They were even more reluctant to hand them back
than the police had been to hand them over the previous day.

As part of our duties, we thought we had better search every building,
so for several mornings and one or two afternoons we went through
hangars and workshops. The airport was large, and had been used for
military as well as civilian purposes. As we set about our task German
Focke-Wolfe fighters flew in from time to time and landed near the control
tower. The pilots clambered out of their planes and walked straight into
the control tower entrance. We made no move to stop or question them,
and never saw them again once they were in their mess. No doubt others
were responsible for them. We were only non-commissioned Army types.
The pilots were responding to a call for all German airforces to surrender
and fly their machines to the nearest airbase occupied by the Allies. The
war was not yet officially over, but the general ceasefire could not be long
delayed.

We explored the hangars and sheds around the airport perimeter. It was
absorbing. We felt like little boys scrumping apples with the farmer safely
away. In one hangar was a Heinkel 111 – no doubt one of the bombers
that had flown over on our recent advance and scared me. The Heinkel
111s had also taken a prominent part in the Battle of Britain. By 1944
it was rather outdated, and no match for the Allied fighters. We climbed
into the machine and explored the cockpit, the rear gunner's position, and
where the bomb aimer lay, and the various pieces of equipment. As those
who had been at the receiving end of death from the sky we were very
interested to see how it felt from the inside. It was very cramped: as bad
if not worse than being cooped up in a tank. To get into the tail gunner's
position was a feat of dexterity worthy of an agile sardine. We tumbled
out, glad that we were not German bomber crews. In another hangar was
an ME 110, a fighter-bomber. We did not explore this closely as it seemed
to have loaded bomb racks, and we feared a booby trap. In every building
we looked for Lugers, but none was to be found. But I picked up a Beretta

What a scruffy lot! Taken as the war ended, May 1945.

CMOS in Berlin. Dennis Bould is second from the left, middle row. The author is crouching at front, first left. Note the newly issued campaign ribbons.

machine pistol and a small Italian automatic. The former I handed in, but the latter I kept, with twenty rounds of ammunition. This was to be an object of admiration for some, but it was also an article of near disaster.

Time was on our hands. I cannot recall anything about our feeding arrangements, but I suppose our own cooks collected rations from a supply unit somewhere. I used to have several photographs, now sadly lost, taken of members of our unit when at the aerodrome. There was one with Sgt Lloyd and a couple of us taken in front of a recently landed Focke-Wolfe fighter. How proud we were to have come so far and have our picture recorded in front of the spoils of war! To think that the mighty German war machine had been finally brought to a standstill in a crushing defeat! It still seemed a dream.

In 1990 I was to come back to Hamburg on a business trip. I was scheduled to fly from the airport to City Airport in London. It looked rather different to when I had spent time there in 1945. There was a new control tower and the entrance and reception were huge and busy with passengers. There were many airline offices and a number of modern passenger planes on the ground, either parked or waiting to take off. But, yes, one or two of the old hangars were still there.

Back to May 1945. After a few days occupying the airport we moved off, crossed the Elbe and drove through devastated Hamburg. The docks and steel works were twisted girders and piles of rubble. The streets were lined with rubble, cleared by pale and poorly-dressed civilians to make way for the convoys of military vehicles passing through. It was not only the slave workers who looked under-nourished. As we drove out of the ruined city, target of several huge bombing raids, and into the countryside of Holstein, we passed hundreds of German soldiers trudging south to surrender in the city. We took little notice of them and they took little notice of us. It was no time for jeering. We had seen too much of war for that sort of thing. The enemy soldiers were dust-stained and silent. There were also some large diesel wagons, heavily laden with men, and some horse-drawn vehicles. Most of the men would have been glad the war was over, and all of them would have been glad to be captured by the British and not by the Russians.

Just outside Itzehoe, a town distinguished by its cement factories, we halted and turned into a field. 'Grub up!' came the cry after an hour of preparation. The afternoon sun began to sink slowly to the west. It was 6 May, and we heard on the radio that all hostilities had ceased. The surrender of the German Army had been officially signed on Lüneburg Heath. There was no holding us. A group decided to drive to the Keil Canal just to have look, and be able to say that they had reached it. Two truckloads took off and drove up to the canal, cheering. There it was, just a canal, with two gun emplacements guarding the bridge over it.

'Let's go on to Flensburg,' said one.

'What's the point of going to Flensburg?' exclaimed another. 'Why not drive to Denmark? It can't be far away.'

But the most insistent said, 'Let's get back to camp before it gets too dark to find our way, and have some drinks.' This proved to be the majority opinion.

On the way back, several of the lads were determined to force their way into a German home and demand drinks to celebrate the victory. I felt uneasy over this, not knowing what might develop. However, the driver of the truck was determined to carry out the diversion, and since he was at the wheel we went with him. He drove off the road up to a farmhouse. The door was heavily locked.

'Open up, we are English soldiers. Englishen Soldaten. Verstehen Sie?' someone said. The door opened slowly, to reveal a very nervous farmer. The crowd pushed into the small entrance hall.

'Bringen Sie Wein und glasses. What the hell is German for glasses?' None of us seemed to know.

The ringleader forced open the door that led to the parlour. Behind the table stood the farmer's wife, looking terrified and surely suspecting the worst. So too was her husband. 'Shush!' he entreated, 'Kinder schlaffen.' And he pointed to the ceiling, to indicate that his children were asleep upstairs.

I could feel that some of my companions were aroused by the sight of the woman. The situation became increasingly tense. Glasses were brought, and a bottle of wine. The wine was poured. 'Here's a toast,' cried the driver, his eyes on the woman. 'Victory to the British and to hell with Hitler. Drink!' he commanded the German couple.

They obediently drank, shaking with fear. Were they to be murdered? Was his wife to be raped?

'More wine!' commanded the driver, his eyes riveted on the woman.

'Shush,' said the man, in an agony of apprehension, 'my children.'

'Never mind your bleeding children, more wine, schnell, schnell!'

More wine was produced and poured. I looked around the six soldiers squeezed into the small room. How many felt as I did that it was time to go? 'Come on,' I said, 'You've had your fun. Let's leave them in peace. They've got youngsters in bed asleep. Let's get back to our camp.'

'No, not yet,' growled the driver. 'I want more wine and another toast.'

With luck, I thought, we might get him away. It did not seem that many of the others were determined on rape and pillage.

'Drink to the end of the Nazis and may all Fräuleins be willing,' leered the driver.

'OK, let's head for home,' said another lad, 'John's right, we've had our fun. Enough is enough.'

We pushed the driver out of the door as he protested, 'You silly, weak-kneed buggers. We could all have had a screw of that bint.'

'Yes, I expect you're right, but we're going back to base now, and don't crash the truck.'

The driver was not very steady, but got into the vehicle and pulled out his rifle. 'I'll put a couple of shots through his window. I'll teach him to have a beautiful wife.'

'Don't be a bloody fool! Do you want to have the blood of innocent children on your hands?'

Slowly the driver put the rifle down. Still protesting, he engaged gear and we regained the road.

I had made an enemy of that driver. For many weeks he scowled at me whenever we met, and once when out on a training exercise later on, I found that someone had interfered with the engine of my 15 cwt Chevrolet truck so that I could not get it started. Eventually I got it going but later that day, when I was talking to one of the bombardiers about the engine, he checked the spark plugs and found they had been connected in the wrong firing order. It must have been the driver's petty revenge.

Back at base, several of the men were lying drunk and unconscious on the grass. The dew was forming over them. Among them was our sergeant. One man was steadily firing his Sten gun in the air until all his ammunition was gone, and uttering a series of cowhand 'whoopees' as he fired. We all joined in with our weapons, shooting them into the gathering night like Afghan tribesmen.

Across the road was a field with a large haystack. 'Come on, lads, let's have a victory bonfire!' someone said. The haystack was duly lit, and a dozen or more soldiers danced round it. In the excitement I flung my fore-and-aft cap into the air and then into the fire.

'Look,' I cried, 'I've burned my cap to celebrate victory!' It seems stupid now, but it seemed absolutely right at the time, and I was relieved that we had extricated ourselves from a potentially horrific situation in the farmhouse.

In the morning there were a number of sore heads, including that of Maj. Crane, who had locked himself in his caravan and drunk himself into a stupor. The telephone wires were hanging in tatters where the victory salvoes the night before had shot into the air.

The next day we were cleaning up, washing our vehicles and generally making do and mending. After our midday meal some of us gathered to yarn. I produced the automatic pistol that I had found in the airport and showed it to my companions.

'You're sure it's not loaded?' asked one of our bombardiers.

'Yes,' I replied, 'I'm quite sure of that.' I pulled the trigger to prove it, pointing to the bombardier's stomach. There was a click, which proved my point.

'You should never point a gun at anyone, whether it's loaded or not. You know how this has been drummed into us ever since we've been in the Army,' remonstrated one of my pals.

'You're right,' I said, and turning away, I pointed the gun to a space between the group and pulled the trigger again. There was a sharp report and a bullet winged its way into the bushes.

'You bloody fool, you could have killed me!' shouted the bombardier.

Shamefaced, I apologised, and walked to the edge of the field and flung the offending gun into the thick hedgerow. I had been lucky once again; or was Providence looking after me? I had certainly learned my lesson over guns. Had I shot the innocent bombardier in the stomach I would have been on a court martial, and almost certainly spent time in a military prison. The authorities were hot on possession of illegal arms. How stupid I had been.

An apology

The war being over, there was no need for the CMOS. Its members had to be deployed elsewhere, but before we knew of our postings we were moved to a clubhouse on the banks of the River Elbe above Hamburg. It was called Fahrhaus Schülau, and had belonged to a sailing club. Its furniture and fittings were quite splendid. After what we had been used to in recent months it was luxury indeed. There was a resident cook and some resident young ladies. Several were from Baltic countries and had fled the oncoming Russians, preferring the Germans to the Russkies (as we learned, from the Germans, to call them). All troops had been ordered not to fraternise with the German civilians. But what of these women? We were unsure of their status. Did they count as German? Were they waitresses? Were they good-time girls? Were they waitresses *and* good-time girls? Some of us were able to find out. I suppose we were in the clubhouse for some time.

Dennis and I made the acquaintance of a one-armed local yachtsman who had been a soldier in the First World War and had lost his arm in battle. He told us in very fair English that he had been a member of the Social Democratic Party, and had spent some time in a concentration camp because of his political views. You can see that the ban on fraternising was largely ignored. He had approached us in the first place and it seemed to us to be uncivilised to ignore him. We asked if we could borrow a rowing boat. He did not possess one but he took us to a boatkeeper who obliged. I can't remember whether we gave him anything for the hire. Perhaps some cigarettes, for they were at a premium in postwar Germany. Even cigarette ends (Stummels) were gathered together and rewrapped for sale.

Dennis and I went back to the clubhouse and proposed a plan. We would row across the Elbe to the other side and back again. The boat had room for six, with two to row and one to steer. Six of us set off in great spirits.

We rowed across the Elbe quite easily; it was, I suppose, about a mile and a half wide at the point where we were stationed. We clambered ashore and looked around for a while. There were acres of fruit trees, and bells were suspended in the branches to frighten the birds. The bells made pleasant music. We had heard them faintly from the other shore. Now that we had landed by them, the noise was a gentle but permanent and unmistakable tinkle.

It was time to go back. We pushed the boat into the water, arranged turns for rowing, and set out for our own shore. By now the tide was running out into the distant sea. We had to pull against the tide to prevent being swept downstream. Pull hard! Pull hard! Rowers became exhausted and had to be changed. Slowly and painfully we held our course homewards. When we reached the middle of the river we ran onto a sandbank. Some jumped out into the soft sand and pushed the boat forward. Others used the oars to push the boat along. We were not making any progress. Someone had to

Victorious leaders on display in Berlin, 1945.

get into the water and pull the boat. We all got out, except the steersman. We pushed and pulled in two feet of water, our feet treading down into the soft sand. An oar slipped into the water and began to float away. 'Get that oar, somebody!' Somebody went after it and went up to his neck in the water. The oar drifted away. We cleared the sandbank and the swift current abated. Soon we reached our shore, to sighs of relief. Six tired and stiff soldiers stepped onto land.

That was not the end of my adventures when at Fahrhaus Schülau. We were talking again to the one-armed ex-soldier, and he suggested that we might sail with him to the other shore. There was an elderly gentleman who wanted to meet British soldiers. Dennis was suspicious, but I calmed his fears. Why should it be a trap? Wasn't our sailor friend a victim of the Nazis? Why would he lead us into a trap? So one day we climbed into the yacht and sailed across the Elbe, more swiftly and more safely than we had done earlier in the rowing boat. We persuaded Lt Hopper to issue us with special passes, partly as a record of our intentions, in case we did not get back.

We landed not far from the beach where we had landed before. Our friend took us along a dirt road, through an orchard, and into a large garden. He knocked at the door of the house. After a few moments, the door was opened by a middle-aged woman, who beckoned us in. We were led into a book-lined room with many pictures on the walls, and stands for certificates and busts. The room smelled of stale tobacco smoke and old furnishings. An elderly man and woman stood up. The man came forward, extending his hand. We shook hands rather diffidently. What was this all about?

'My friends,' said our sailor, 'allow me to present Herr Schmidt and his family.'

In halting English and with a strong accent he told us that he had once been in the German diplomatic service under the Kaiser, and had had the honour of representing both his own country and Great Britain in Costa Rica. He said he had also been a joint consul. 'In 1912 I was responsible jointly for German and British interests in Honduras.' By the time he had finished speaking he was sobbing, and turned his head away from embarrassment.

One of the women said, 'You must forgive my father. He was a loyal servant of His Imperial Majesty Wilhelm the Second. He has hated the Nazis and what they have done.' We looked at each other, sharing in the old man's embarrassment.

He picked up some framed documents and showed them to us. 'See, here is the proof of my story. It was an honour to serve King George as well as the Kaiser.'

His daughter added, 'My father has been so unhappy with what the Nazis have done to this country. He wanted to meet you to apologise for all the bad things Hitler has done.'

Emotions were calmed and a bottle and glasses appeared. We drank to the past and to previous and future Anglo-German friendship. Medals were produced and shown with pride to illustrate the former diplomat's credentials. They were all pre-1914. There was more handshaking and more bowing and a further round of Schnapps. We left in a slight haze, not knowing if we had overdone accepting the apologies, not knowing if we had exceeded the bounds of official non-fraternisation orders. But who would know? We knew that the little ceremony had meant much to the frail old gentleman; and to our yachtsman too. He seemed pleased that his task had been accomplished. 'He will die in peace now.'

We kept silent on the way back. When we got back to the clubhouse our colleagues were more sceptical: 'I bet he didn't make a fuss when Hitler was winning the war. He's like all the bloody Germans. When they are on top they kick your face in. When they're down they lick your bloody boots!' But Dennis and I did not see it that way.

In Berlin

Soon we got the exciting news that we were to go with the rest of 7th Armoured Division to Berlin. We would be the first British troops there. It had been Churchill's wish that 7th Armoured should have this honour because of its battle record in the Western Desert and later in Italy and Normandy. There had been a delay in Russia's sharing the occupation of Berlin with the other allies, but after much diplomatic activity Stalin had relented, and contingents from Britain, America and France were to be permitted as fellow occupiers of the capital city. The Division took the road from the Brunswick area and entered the city in July, having been allocated the area around the Olympic Stadium. We began our entry on 19 July. As we moved along the road through the Russian-occupied land we noted the absence of Russian troops. The road went straight through flat, uninteresting farmland. The convoy was stopped from time to time by road checks. As we entered Berlin we saw a notice put up by our advance column: 'This Axis has been laid from El Alamein to Berlin'. It was embellished with the Desert Rat sign of the famous division.

Churchill was determined that the British troops in Berlin should not be disadvantaged by the American or Russian troops, who might already have medal ribbons for the campaign in north-west Europe. As a consequence, we of the 7th Armoured Division were given medal ribbons – in lieu of the 1939-45 Star and the France and Germany Star – before other troops in Germany, and had them sewn onto our tunics during July and August 1945. The medals themselves, with the 1939-45 War Medal, were sent much later by post to our home addresses.

CMOS was allocated accommodation with HQRA in the suburb of Spandau. We had little to do but clean our equipment, smarten ourselves up in general, scrub and whiten our webbing, and be a military presence in the city. It was a good hour's walk from our billets to the centre of Berlin. Once settled in, a group of us began to explore.

The whole of Berlin was open to the military. There were as yet no zones for the four occupying powers. British, American, French and Russian soldiers could intermingle. A big NAAFI called the Winston Club was opened in the British sector. Into this canteen, soldiers from the four armies used to flock for 'char and wads'. We were very interested in the Russian soldiers, since they were an unknown quantity, and they were held in great esteem by the Allies because of their fight against the Nazis. There was strong goodwill between the Allies and the Russians at that time. That goodwill was soon to be dissipated. I met one private of the Red Army in the club. He was smartly dressed (most Russian soldiers were not) and spoke good English. He was, in fact, a Pole, who had joined the Red Army and had been on the personal staff of a general in command of an infantry division. The division had marched all the way from Stalingrad to Berlin, fighting as they travelled, a distance of something like 1,300 miles. They had little transport and made what use they could of abandoned or captured German vehicles. This Pole was a linguist, as had been the Yugoslav officer. He could speak Russian, English and German. We were all very impressed.

Other Russians soldiers were less impressive. All except senior officers wore a smock over their trousers, a belt, and strong leather boots not unlike German jackboots. They wore peaked caps, or fore-and-aft hats rather like our own. Officers and other ranks mixed together more informally than ours did. The officers wore shoulder tabs with their arm and rank indicated in gold on red. Once on duty, the discipline was harsh. They had long hours of guard duty and any slackness was severely punished. Death was not an uncommon sentence for what in our army would have been a relatively mild offence. I thought of my falling asleep at Rauray and was glad I was not serving in the Red Army. On one occasion, however, I witnessed an extraordinary incident. A Russian Jeep pulled up at the side of a city street; an officer alighted and entered a building. A few minutes later he re-emerged and climbed into the Jeep. He lit a cigarette. His driver, who had sat waiting for his officer, leaned across the wheel and after a few moments of argument snatched the cigarette from the officer's mouth and began to smoke it, whereupon the officer snatched it back again and offered the driver a cigarette from his packet. They then drove away without another word.

Once, when it was my tour of duty to be driver for CMOS, I was travelling along a road with burnt-out buildings on each side. As I neared an intersection I spotted a Red Army private staggering from side to side. He was obviously very drunk. I halted the truck and called out to him in my halting German. Could I take him somewhere? German was the only tongue in which the British and Russians could make themselves understood. He scrambled aboard and sat in the passenger seat. 'Ja, Bahnhof.' I indicated that I wanted to see his papers, which he was clutching in his hand. He had a fistful of Russian banknotes and a pass. I looked at the pass to see what railway station he wanted. I could not read it. He took a bottle of vodka from his pocket (he had another sticking out of his pack), and offered me a drink. Having wiped the neck of the bottle, I obliged him with a swig. I passed the bottle back to him and started to drive in the direction of what I hoped was the nearest station.

'Ich gehe Heimat,' he said, hiccoughing. 'Ich gehe nach Haus. Meine Mutter und mein Vater.'

'Are you being demobbed?'

'Ich gehe nach Haus. Seit drei Jahren ich habe Soldaten sein.'

I asked him where he lived. He said near Moscow. So he had been paid off, given a pass and left to find his own way home. Well, that was a revelation. Compared to our own meticulous movement orders with our ticket, pass, train itinerary, and pick-up and put-down points, their system was crude. I stopped near a rail terminus and bade him farewell. Was the station operational? Would there be a train going to Moscow? Would he perhaps make his own way on foot, hitching lifts? We shook hands and he warmly embraced me. He smelt of vodka imbibed over several days. 'Tovarich! Comrade! Kamerad!' We parted, he near to tears, me not sorry to get rid of him. I hope he did get back home eventually.

The centre of Berlin was devastated, and most of the outer districts were also badly damaged. Grand official buildings, hotels, department stores and apartments were in ruins or starkly burnt out. As duty driver I had the opportunity to drive around the city. I found the famous Unter den Linden and the Wilhelmstrasse. Somewhere in the Wilhelmstrasse was the Reich Chancellery, where Hitler had his official residence when in Berlin.

With Dennis and George Laidlaw, I drove the truck up to the entrance to the Chancellery. A Russian sentry saluted from a sentry box. We got out of the truck and returned the salute. The sentry did not try to stop us. Did he think because we had arrived in a truck that we were important? In the courtyard was the burnt-out remains of a German scout car. We crunched over broken glass and debris and entered the main doors. Where did we go now? From the entrance hall rose a wide and elegant staircase. The walls were pitted with bullet marks and the smell of brick and cement dust hung heavily, although the fighting for the building had ceased seven weeks earlier.

At the top of the stairs was a corridor from the landing. At the end of the corridor was a large double door. We pushed the door open and entered. We were in the famous hall of mirrors, which I had seen on the newsreels back home. This was where Hitler had received Mussolini, where Molotov had been met by Hitler, and where many diplomats and statesmen had flitted across the newsreels in the last ten years. Now it was no longer the elegant reception hall. The mirrors, which had been fitted from top to bottom, were smashed and trampled by Russian boots. The soldiers had fired their Tommy guns all along the walls, bringing down the plaster and the expensive glass. At the far end of the former hall of mirrors was another double door. We opened it and found ourselves in Hitler's study.

There was a large empty desk covered with dust. A huge ornamental chandelier hung low from the ceiling. Beyond the desk was a broad window, through which could be seen a small courtyard. It was Hitler's study for sure, because we all recognised it from newsreels and newspapers. From here Hitler had planned and plotted the rise and fall of the Third Reich. Here had been Goering, Himmler, Hess, Goebbels, Ribbentrop, Schacht and the other Nazi leaders. We moved to the window and looked into the courtyard. A brick wall some twelve feet high surrounded it. In one corner were the remains of a bonfire. The wall at that point was smoke-blackened by the burning. We left the room feeling exultant. We had reached the heart of Hitler's Germany.

We walked along other corridors and into a succession of offices. Here numerous secretaries had typed and filed at the command of the Führer. Ranged along the walls and jutting out into the offices were filing cabinets upon filing cabinets of personnel. There were cards of party members neatly filed and indexed. I took one as a souvenir, now lost after these many years. On one shelf, a stack of cards inviting someone to have breakfast with the Führer. The name was left blank for insertion. We helped ourselves to some of these. As a final memento I picked up a typewriter brush, for the obscure reason that it would remind me of our adventure each time I cleaned my webbing with it. On the way out we paused at a small doorway that must have led down to the basement. Should we go down and explore further? We did not have a torch and, furthermore, there might be a booby trap. A vision of a Panzer Faust primed to blow our heads off when the door was opened made us draw back. No doubt the Russians would have explored below, but we hesitated and moved on. Had we known, we might have been the first British troops to enter the war operations room, the underground bunker where Hitler and Eva Braun had committed suicide.

What happened in the bunker was investigated and reconstructed by Hugh Trevor-Roper in his book *The Last Days of Hitler*. Had he been there before us? Or did he come afterwards? The smoke-blackened courtyard was where Hitler's body had been burned by his devoted guards after his suicide. We had seen this, but not realised at the time its significance. When I returned to the Chancellery some days later with other soldiers to do some more exploring and take photographs, there were British military police on guard with the Russians, and we were turned away: 'No admittance except to intelligence officers and officers above the rank of major.' But we, a lance bombardier and two gunners, had already been there.

Berlin had been a beautiful city. It is now. My wife and I have travelled to Berlin twice recently and were surprised by its restoration. In 1945, it was ruined and in economic and social chaos. Food was desperately short for the civilians. The value of money had plummeted to zero. The means of exchange was the cigarette. Every day a black market congregated near the shell-pocked Brandenburg Gate, where Berliners would come with their surviving possessions and trade them for cigarettes. A camera could be bartered for fifty cigarettes, a gold wristwatch for forty; a woman's body could be obtained for as little as ten. It would be better for her if she became a soldier's lover for as long as he was in Berlin, as she would get food and protection against Russian soldiers out to rape. The supply of food was regulated by the military according to each zone. The Russian high command had done a good job in assessing the numbers living in Berlin and supplying the details to the other occupiers. Food did come through to the half-starved civilians but it was meagre. The entire economic and transport system of the Third Reich had broken down.

The Berliners feared the Russians and almost regarded the British as saviours. Not only had they had to endure street fighting and destruction of their buildings district by district, but the Russian soldiers engaged in systematic rape. More than one British Tommy shacking up with his Fräulein had been heard to say, 'We fought the wrong war. We should have been on the Germans' side against the Russkies.' Such was the fear and enmity of the women of Berlin. The non-fraternisation law was speedily eroded, and was repealed after several months. It was unenforceable. Moreover, the Allied authorities wanted to get German civilians working for them to develop a new democratic country.

There were other pastimes for our soldiers. A series of lakes lay to the west of the city. These had been pleasure resorts for Berliners. Now they became pleasure resorts for Allied soldiers. Dennis and I spent many

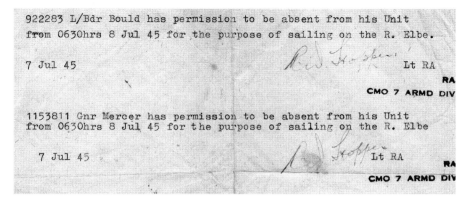

922283 L/Bdr Bould has permission to be absent from his Unit
from 0630hrs 8 Jul 45 for the purpose of sailing on the R. Elbe.

7 Jul 45   Lt RA

                                                              RA

                                              CMO 7 ARMD DIV

1153811 Gnr Mercer has permission to be absent from his Unit
from 0630hrs 8 Jul 45 for the purpose of sailing on the R. Elbe

7 Jul 45   Lt RA

                                                              RA

                                              CMO 7 ARMD DIV

Passes issued to Dennis and the author, 7 July 1945.

happy hours on the lake. We went canoeing in a kayak and soon mastered the double-sided paddles. Had we not mastered the Elbe with oars? A steam-driven lake steamer filled with boozy soldiers, singing and laughing, chugged its way across the Wansee. The German operators and the staff of the lakeside club, which had been reopened for our men, seemed to enjoy our good spirits as much as we did. I suppose they were used to seeing their own young soldiers doing the same thing. Every German loves a soldier, it has been said. A Scottish pipe band from the 51st Highland Division paraded one day, and marched along some of the cleared streets between rows of apartments. Many civilians came out to watch and to cheer. On 21 July there was a victory parade along the straight road through the Tiergarten. Units from the 7th Armoured Division, from the American, from the French, and from the Russians, paraded their tanks, guns and foot soldiers. The CMOS contingent lined the route of the parade. The parade was led by the victorious leaders: Churchill, Truman, De Gaulle and, in lieu of Stalin, General Zhukov. The sun shone, the bands played, and the Allies tried to outshine each other with their martial bearing and marching. We had had a rehearsal on a previous day, so all went well. I was privileged to be in the line and to see the famous war leaders pass by, and to compare the appearance of the passing troops.

Soon the Allies organised games against each other. The Olympic Stadium, last used in 1936, was brought into use. Many of the races and field events were rehearsed, and on the great day Marlene Dietrich arrived to bring some glamour to the occasion. She looked young, but was well into middle age. Her million-dollar legs were much admired when she presented the prizes and signed autographs. The Russians did not take part. I cannot remember what the excuse was, but we all knew that they

25 pounders of 3rd RHA taking part in the victory parade in Berlin.

could not provide suitable sporting gear for their team. In the event, the Americans won. The score was: America ninety-four points, Britain forty-three points, France twenty-five points.

During this period (about six weeks) I joined with two other soldiers, Peter Boot and Wally Coldrick, to set up a forces' newspaper. Peter had been a trainee journalist. Wally was a commercial artist. We were encouraged by our brigadier. We called it the *Berlin Bugle*, and it ran for six editions. Boot proved to be a whizzkid at locating German printers and paper wholesalers. In our first edition there was a brilliant cartoon executed by Wally in the style of Giles. It showed two husky, macho soldiers (like Bluto in Popeye) looking at a poster advertising entertainments. One says to the other, 'What shall it be tonight, Beethoven, ballet, booze or bints?'

Peter managed to get some glamour photographs for the front page. This was good publicity for the newspaper. There was no charge for it. A major problem was how many numbers to print, and where to distribute them. We took some to the Winston Club and to any other forces' canteens in our sector. We took some to the black market area around the Brandenburg Gate and handed them out. We arrived in a jeep carrying a big notice, 'Forces' Newspaper'. The authorities in the meantime had cracked down on black marketing and any obvious exchanges could lead to arrest by military police, so the crowds were much thinner.

We reported on the 'Olympic Games', on the black market, on any gossip, on the opening of a new lakeside club by Mary Churchill; and we published readers' letters. Peter and I did the reporting between us, and Wally did the cartoons and illustrations. We had a lot of fun. I do not recall that we were ever censored, but I seem to recall the CRA did call us to his office to query the propriety of something we had written. When we left Berlin in October, Peter Boot must have been posted to another unit, for I never saw him again. Wally Coldrick kept turning up wherever I went, but I think he, too, was posted away from me.

One day, after a few of us had been to the Catholic soldiers' club near a major railway station, we saw some emaciated German soldiers standing at the street corner. They were dressed in tattered Wehrmacht uniforms, and their boots were worn right through. One was barefooted, with straw wrapped round his bleeding feet. My anger at what the Germans had done to people of other countries, and the appalling way the Nazis had acted towards the Jews, evaporated at the sight of these men. They had obviously been on the Russian front and had been prisoners, now released and come home to Berlin. As with my drunken Russian soldier, they had to find their own way back. The Russians could hardly treat their enemies better than their own men released from military service. 'Look at those half-starved Jerries over there,' I said. 'They're skin and bone. Shall we buy them some food from the club?'

My companions were uncertain. 'Suppose someone sees us? We might get into trouble.'

'Why should we get into trouble? Come on, I'm going to get something for them.'

Only one of my companions joined me. The others looked on disapprovingly. We got some doughnuts and took them over to the gaggle of men. They thanked us and wolfed them down. We never saw them again. Did they find their homes in Berlin? Did they find a heap of rubble? Were their loved ones still alive? These men were a microcosm of the hundreds of thousands of former enemies trying to return to find a home.

Our departure from Berlin was imminent. There was a frenzy of packing and preparation. The bombardier waiter for the officers' mess was taken ill. Someone had to be found to take charge of the mess during the move, and be responsible for the wine cellar. For some reason I could never fathom I was approached by the mess secretary and asked if I would take the job on until such time as the bombardier returned to duty. I said that I would. After all, it would be a new experience, and I might learn how the other half lived.

The night before we left, a whole crowd of us went down to a Bierkeller to celebrate our departure from Berlin. I had to be up and ready to lead the truck containing the mess drink at 5 a.m. We were drinking Steinhager, a local gin, from stoneware bottles. Gin and orange was a popular tipple, and I liked it as well as anyone. My glass was filled and refilled a couple of times, and then I insisted that only orange juice should be added. I was aware of a good deal of smiling and amusement and put it down to the happy atmosphere. Then my head began to swim. I got up quietly and went to the lavatory. I began to feel terrible. I thought I was going to pass out. Those rotten mates of mine, or some of them, had been trying to get me drunk. They had been filling my glass with neat gin when I wasn't looking. Perhaps some had thought this a good way to get at the officers. Some may have resented that I was going to be the mess waiter. One even might have been getting his own back for spoiling his rape in the farmhouse as the war ended. Maybe I was seen to be too uppity in editing the *Berlin Bugle*. Who knows? I put my forehead against the cold concrete wall of the urinal and fought to gain a hold on myself. I would not oblige them and pass out. I would walk out into the evening air and go straight back to my billet and make sure I was awakened at 4 a.m. in order to be early to move off at 5 a.m. I left the urinal and walked off without saying a word to anyone. At 5 a.m. the next day I climbed into the passenger seat of the truck and told the driver to move off and follow the vehicle in front. I felt weary, but not drunk. No one ever mentioned the previous night to me, and I said nothing about it. It was best treated that way.

Promotion – and a new career

I arrived at the village of Albersdorf, not far from Hamburg. The CRA and his staff were lodged in a large house. The wine was established in the cellar. I had a book to record wine taken out and taken in. I dispensed the drinks under the orders of the mess officer. I waited the tables at evening dinner and learned not to add my own conversation to that of the diners. I nominally supervised two cooks, a charming Danish couple who had been engaged for the task.

There were several German workers at the house. One was an energetic lad who had been a member of a U-boat crew, and he told me that he had seen the Statue of Liberty through the periscope. Once discharged, he had not known what to do, and had attached himself to the household in order to get a little food. He spent most of the time chopping wood. He received no pay from the mess funds and was regarded as yet another hanger-on. Another was a girl refugee from Silesia, who had attached herself to the Danish couple. She had fled as the Red Army advanced, and had witnessed and been involved in terrible situations. When asked about her experiences she would shake her head and say 'Furchtbar!' ('Dreadful'). Since the British army had food, there were many Germans who hung around trying to get some kind of job. There had been one smooth-talking civilian, in a well-cut suit, who had fastened himself on to HQRA in Berlin and made himself, in his own view, indispensable to the officers on account of his good English and knowledge of the business community of the city. He was regarded as a pain by most of the officers, and when he was found stealing from Army stores and dealing in the black market with Army rations, he was dumped on the roadside outside Berlin as the convoy left for Albersdorf. Protesting his innocence to the end, he vanished behind us as we sped along the Autobahn to the west.

After a week or so I received my marching orders. The CMOS was wound up and all personnel were dispersed to various units. Dennis Bould and I were to meet for the last time in a steamy café in the town. I was put on regimental guard duty, the first time since leaving England for the invasion. I had to smarten myself up and ensure that all the webbing was well scrubbed and the brasses clean. I was sent as ceremonial guard at the HQ house where the day before I had been the mess steward.

A week later I was delivered to 'J' Battery of the 3rd Regiment of the Royal Horse Artillery, stationed in the market town of Elmshorn. I was once more a driver/operator with a regular artillery unit equipped with 25 pounders hauled by quads. The first thing that happened was being told to unpick the crossed flags sewn on my battledress that indicated I was a signaller. 'We don't wear things like that in the RHA. You can get some brass shoulder badges from the stores that will tell the rest of the Army that you are in a crack regiment!' Next I was told to blanco my webbing white. The Royal Horse Artillery had two regiments in the Normandy Campaign, the 3rd and the 5th. They were friendly rivals, but there was a long-standing antipathy between the RHA and the Brigade of Guards. This may have gone back many years over the honour of being 'Right of the Line'. In the past this antipathy had led to brawls and pub fights. Certainly, the RHA members felt their superiority when among fellow gunners.

I had not been long in Elmshorn before I made friends with a refugee from Latvia. Our guns were parked in the grounds of a leather factory, and I came across the manager, Rupert Masting. He was married to Irina, a beautiful woman from Siberia. They had a three-year-old son, Peter. Rupert's father had been the owner of a leather factory in Riga. Rupert was a chemical expert. The factory had been taken over by the Soviets when they invaded the Baltic States in 1940. Rupert had not liked the Russian occupation and the way the factory was reorganised, and when the Germans drove out the Russians in 1941 they got the factory back to the way it had been. Then when the Russians came back, driving the Germans out, he fled with the German Army and got the job in Elmshorn. They lived in a tiny house within the factory complex. I was invited to spend Christmas with them. Rupert had a little English; Irena had none. Peter was picking up English from the soldiers, swearwords mostly, and German from the local children. Rupert complained that the German children spoke 'bad' German. He seemed to care less about the English swearing. We had a modest but tasty Christmas dinner and sat beside a tiny Christmas tree. It was a spot of home comfort much appreciated. Since it was the German custom to celebrate the festival on Christmas Eve, I was not surprised to hear the church bells ring at midnight. To hear voices singing 'Holy Night' reminded me that despite the Nazis, many Germans were practising Christians. The German tongue can often sound harsh and guttural, but when sung, German sounds beautiful.

Mrs Masting and the author celebrating Christmas in Elmshorn, 1945.

The author with Peter Masting in the tanning factory yard.

Rupert wanted to come to Britain. I asked my mother to find a trade paper that covered the leathermaking industry. Before long a trade paper arrived by post, and through it Rupert found a job in Clackmannanshire, and after a while moved to Scotland. For several years afterwards we corresponded, but eventually the contact died. If Peter is still alive he would be in his late sixties. I wonder how he got on in his new land, and what his memories would be.

The older soldiers were being released from the Army. I was Group 46, which meant I had to wait at least until December 1946; another year. I remember one sad farewell. One of our sergeants had been living with a German girl. They were very much in love. This was no casual affair. When his demobilisation came through, she begged him to stay. But he had a wife and family at home, and these came first with him. They parted in sorrow and the woman was distraught. I can still see him leaving her and walking away down the road, leaving her in floods of tears.

One day when I was duty driver I was told to take one of our sergeant-majors to Hanover to catch an aeroplane to England, as his daughter was seriously ill. This flight would have been on an RAF transport plane, probably a Dakota. Hanover was some distance away, about 100 miles to the south-west. I must have consulted a map and taken it with me. There were few existing road signs, but once having got through Hamburg I got onto an Autobahn and reached some barracks in Hanover before dark. My passenger was driven away, and I found some food and looked for a bed for the night. No bed was found, so I slept on the polished floor of a barrack block with a single blanket. I was cold and uncomfortable. At dawn I stretched my aching limbs and got some breakfast. As I returned to the truck to go back to Elmshorn I saw with a thrill of horror that I had a flat front tyre. I looked for the spare and could not find one. I had left without checking that I had a spare tyre. I would be in trouble when I reported in; but my immediate problem was getting my tyre repaired. There were no workshops at the barracks, but a friendly voice said that just down the road was a German tyre factory, and I could get fixed up there. I drove on my flat tyre for over a mile and pulled in to the forecourt.

It took me several attempts to make the Germans understand what needed to be done. At last they got the message and took the tyre off the wheel replaced the inner tube and fixed the wheel back on again. I thanked them and drove off. I had gone barely a mile when the tyre went flat gain. Was this inferior workmanship, or was it a deliberate attempt to sabotage me? I drove on, desperately hoping to see an Army unit that had a workshop attached. Before long I was rewarded, and pulled into a tank-repair troop of the Ordnance Corps. The sergeant said that he had to finish repairing a tank, and then he would take a look at my problem. I got something to eat and waited. By midday the tank repair was finished and he and his men gave me a new tyre, as the old one was badly ripped. Off I went back to Elmshorn, travelling fast along the Autobahn; but my troubles were not yet over. As I sped along I hit a hole in the road where a whole section of the concrete surface had dropped down. I came down with a great bump and the engine cut out. Upon examination it proved nothing worse than the sparking plug leads being forced off with the impact. Once more connected up, the engine fired and I was able to proceed. On the way I picked up a German policeman who was hitchhiking to Hamburg. I dropped him off after a while and entered the parking place I had left the day before. I reported to the duty officer, who asked me if the sergeant-major had got off all right. No questions were asked about my long absence. No one knew about the missing spare tyre. As soon as I could I placed a new spare tyre in the truck. I was not going to be caught lacking again.

In the canteen I noticed an attractive German girl serving at the till. She spoke good English. Unlike a number of the lads, I was not one for casual sex. I watched her for several evenings, then spoke to her and asked if she could help me to improve my German. Her name was Anneliese Otto. She was a young widow, her husband, a seaplane pilot, having been shot down off the coast of Denmark towards the end of the war. They had not been married long. She confessed to me that she had been a member of the Hitler Youth, and later became a nurse and had been with the German Army in Yugoslavia when they were fighting the partisans. I think we had two lessons of German. I cannot think where we met. We liked each other but never touched. Or did I kiss her hand and make her blush? It was a tender relationship. What might have been more romantic was cut short when we moved out of Elmshorn – but we were to meet again.

We left Elmshorn and moved to Oldenburg, close to the Dutch border. Oldenburg had been a garrison town, so we moved into the German barracks. This was an unpopular move, as a guard was mounted at the gate and all soldiers had to report in and out. We no longer had the freedom to come and go as we pleased. I met with another Mercer, Keith, and we, together with Eric Horton, began another forces' newspaper, *Stand Easy*, and it ran until I left the Army. There must have been at least six editions.

We were well served with films for entertainment. One of the editions of the paper ran a review of films on offer within the space of a fortnight. They were: *The Corn Is Green*, starring Bette Davies; *Lady on a Train*, with Deanna Durbin; *Brief Encounter*, with Celia Johnson and Trevor Howard; *I Know Where I'm Going*, with Wendy Hillier and Roger Livesey; *Lady in the Dark*, with Ginger Rogers; *Saratoga Trunk*, starring Ingrid Bergman and Gary Cooper; and *Meet Me in St Louis*, with Judy Garland. Those were the days when Hollywood ruled, and when the cinema was the major field of entertainment. Television was still in the experimental stage, and its development had been hindered by the war.

It was always a problem to get enough material for each fortnightly edition of the newspaper, and I expect a number of the contributions were put in by the editors. There was a letters column, and here is one on the perennial subject of tea:

Dear Mr Editor,
    The Regimental Canteen serves tea at morning break. But it is tea in name only, as usually one is charged half a mark for a cup of hot, slightly tanned water. This is even putting the railway buffet to shame. Tea had hitherto been free and apart from occasional lapses by the Battery cooks, it has been drinkable. Is this yet another inconvenience of barrack life?
    [Signed] CHAR WALLAH.

One aspect of military service was the mixing of social classes. Many junior officers were grammar school boys, whereas the more senior ones would have been from public schools, although some of the grammar schools produced officers who by ability became seniors. On the other hand, I knew two ordinary gunners from public schools, one of whom had been at Eton as a housemaster. Among the rank and file were men from all social origins, speaking a variety of regional accents. I learned so much about people from my Army days. I had never heard a Geordie voice before, or met a Glaswegian. Men got on well together. They supported one another. In battle they relied upon one another. In Germany immediately after the war, soldier helped soldier – witness the help given to me on my Hanover trip. There was formality and informality. There was great fellowship. To some of the regular soldiers, usually NCOs, the Army was family. They owed everything to the Army, some having been rescued from delinquency by their military service. Men found their friends according to shared interests and values. When I moved to the 3rd RHA I knew no one, but soon made new friends and acquaintances. There was 'Learie' Constantine, George Laidlaw, Jim Pearce and, of course, my two co-editors.

I was not long in Oldenburg before I was called into the battery office by Capt. Cadbury, who asked me to act as intelligence clerk. I explained that I knew little German – how could I do this task? He wanted someone to file reports from others and to keep a watchful eye on civilians. This I did to the best of my ability, but I am sure my contribution to military intelligence was very limited. I was taken out of the battery office to take part in a training exercise on Lüneburg Heath. The CRA was receiving newly qualified officers for England who had not seen the war. He wanted them to have a taste of live firing. I was signaller in a Comet tank, the newest and most powerful tank the British Army had received. I thought it was a great pity that this vehicle had not been available in Normandy to take on and knock out the Tigers. When we got to the firing range, the brigadier called up the first of his young officers. He was given a target. After consulting his map he gave the first fire order: 'HE 119 charge two.'

I repeated the order to the guns.

'Angle of site zero.'

There was a pregnant pause. 'Excuse me, sir,' I called out, 'You have not given the bearing.'

'Oh, bearing zero 126 degrees.'

This I repeated. There was another long pause. 'Give the angle of sight again,' I hissed.

'Angle of sight zero,' he said.

This I repeated to the guns.

'Fire by order.'

'Sir, you need to give the range.'

'Range 3,000.'

The guns received my radio message.

'Troop, ready.'

I passed this to the officer.

'Fire.'

Fire was sent to the guns.

'Add four hundred.'

The bracket was made, the target was centred, and four rounds of gunfire ordered.

The CRA asked another officer to take over. Nervously he looked through his binoculars at the range. The target was a group of abandoned trucks.

'Range 2,600.'

'Excuse me, sir,' I said, 'You need to give the charge first.'

'It seems to me,' said the CRA loudly, 'that only the signaller knows what he is doing.' He did not recognise me as his one-time mess steward, or if he did he made no mention of it.

After the shoot was over, that battery sergeant-major came up to me and asked who I was and where I had come from. He assumed that I had come over as a replacement just before the war ended. I tried to explain that I had been with 185 Field Regiment in 49th Division, but he brushed me aside and went to the CRA.

To my surprise, when a list of gunners to be trained for junior leadership was posted up, my name was on it. Twelve of us from the three batteries were promoted to acting lance-bombardier and began a course of training. I cannot at this distance of time remember just what we did, but it certainly involved a lot of drill, and we had to drill each other. I quite enjoyed this. There were elements of the corps de ballet in 'square-bashing'. I also recall playing tennis with a German coach.

At the end of the course we were all confirmed in the rank of lance-bombardier and I received a few more pence in my pay. The responsibility was not overwhelming. I was required from time to time to be the NCO in charge of the marching relief. This meant I was second-in-command of a guard duty under a sergeant, and I had to lead the next guard out to his post, make sure he knew his duties, and then march the former guard back to the guardroom. It meant little sleep when on duty, and I was responsible for ensuring that the guard was correctly dressed and alert throughout the night. I also had to be on the ready for an orderly officer, whose job it was to come round to see the guard was effective. You never knew at what time the orderly officer was coming. The slacker ones might not come at all. The really keen ones might turn up at 2 a.m. on a wet night.

There was one unpleasant task that we had to do at the request of the military government. A large number of displaced Yugoslavs were occupying a former camp outside the town. We had orders to remove them, and escort them to trucks to return them to their country. It was Government policy to return all displaced persons to their former homeland. These Yugoslavs had no intention of returning home, as they feared persecution from Tito and his Communist Party. Like the Yugoslavs I had met earlier, they had the misfortune to end the war on the wrong side. When we arrived at the camp we were told to fix bayonets and order them out of the huts. There were men, women and children. 'Do we have to do this, sir?' I said to our officer. He gave no answer. I suspect he hated the task as much as I did. The spokesman for the military government addressed the Yugoslavs who were staying in the huts. After a good deal of parleying they were ordered to leave by the trucks. We loaded our rifles and took aim at the windows. Reluctantly they emerged. They spat at us and cursed us, but they did move. They drove off to what fate we never knew.

The Army made great efforts to prepare soldiers for their return to civilian life. There were lectures on plans for the future in Britain. There were discussions on housing and on the Beveridge Report, which was the blueprint for the National Health Service implemented in 1948. There were also opportunities to go on residential course. I travelled to Ghent on a geography week, which was led by a rather vague but charming major who had been a university lecturer. Among other things, we learned about the vagaries of weather forecasting, and why it was so difficult to predict the weather in north-west Europe.

I had decided that I would not return to Barclays Bank upon my release. I had received food parcels from the bank from time to time and Mr Boutcher, the manager of Ashford, where last I had been a clerk, was disappointed that I did not want to return; but I was resolved to be a teacher. In this I was greatly motivated by Maurice Tyerman and by my feeling that I wanted to do something with children rather than work with dusty figures and other people's money. The Government had launched a scheme to attract service men and women into teaching. There was a shortfall in teachers because of the war. Teaching was not a reserved occupation and the training colleges had been turning out very few teachers in wartime, so the Emergency Training Scheme was launched. New short-term colleges were established to run a one-year course with the emphasis on teaching practice and very few holidays: one year to do what traditionally took two. I applied to join the scheme and was delighted when I was accepted at an interview held somewhere near Victoria Station. I was on leave at the time. Little did I realise that I would have to wait two years after my release before I was able to start the course.

Because of my acceptance into the scheme I was able to attend a week in Göttingen University in Germany run by Sir Mortimer Wheeler, at the time a brigadier in the Army, but well-known as an archaeologist. There were some twenty men on the pre-teaching course, and I made new friends in Fred Skinner and Reg Tollett. Our tutors were former teachers. Capt. Charlesworth had been an elementary school teacher, and Maj. Toswell a housemaster at Rugby. With their different backgrounds, the two made interesting contrasts. All on the course were destined to teach in schools under the new dispensation of the 1944 act. Elementary schools were to be split into primary and secondary modern schools. Most of those on the course would find themselves later in colleges providing training for children aged between nine and fourteen. It was a very happy week. Göttingen was a lovely old town free from any wartime bombing, with an ancient university. It had a statue of the Goose Girl in the town square, as a memorial to the Brothers Grimm, who composed their fairytales while professors at the university. We had an excursion to the Harz Mountains and listened to a classical music performance. Fred Skinner was well versed in this field; I was a learner; Reg Tollett was lowbrow and did not attend.

Back at Oldenburg I was in the battery office doing very little. I had had a week's leave (I suppose this was when I was interviewed for the Emergency Training Scheme). When I returned from that leave I was told, somewhat frigidly by my namesake Keith, that a Fraülein had come to see me. This must have been Anneliese. She had travelled all the way from Elmshorn to Oldenburg, involving several train changes, to see me. I was surprised, flattered, disappointed I had not seen her, and at the same time alarmed that our brief acquaintance should have meant so much to her.

The battery major came to see me. He was an abrupt, short-tempered man who had joined the Army as a boy bugler and worked his way up to become a major, and in a crack regiment where most of the officers were upper middle class. He was rightly proud of his achievement, but it made him sensitive about his position. He told me there was to be a training scheme. He wanted me as his signaller, and out of the office, where I was wasting my time. 'I can make you the signals sergeant if you decide to stay on.' This was a prospect to be considered, for I knew it would be some time until I could enter college. But the thought of my mother, who had forgone my support for nearly five years, decided me against it.

The scheme started. The major was in a bad mood because he had to travel in a Bren carrier and not a tank. The tank had been disallowed by superior orders on the grounds of economy. There was to be a mock engagement with 'foreign' troops, and fire orders had to be sent. It was a wet day and we were operating in dense pinewoods. Try as I could, I was not able to transmit. The radio was unable to make contact. I re-netted several times in the hope of getting through, but to no avail. The major was beside himself with anger. The practice was a total failure, and I was to blame. 'You deliberately ruined the exercise. You failed to contact on purpose. You wanted to stay in your bloody little office rather than come out on real soldiering. I shan't forget this, bombardier!'

I tried to explain that I had done my best, that the radio did not work well, if at all, in woodlands, and that the wet weather had not helped; but the major was adamant that I was the cause of the failure. I felt very angry too. My competence and pride in efficiency was ridiculed. On return I spoke with an officer who was trying to set up a local school for the incoming children of servicemen's families. Just as soldiers were being released from the Army and going home, others newly called up were replacing them in the army of occupation, and some were bringing their families.

The officer, another major, shook his head. 'Don't worry. I know he is short-tempered. He will forget all about it by tomorrow. I have something else for you to do. I need some teachers for the school I am setting up. I know you will be training to be a teacher back home. Can you help? You will be made up to sergeant.' How could I refuse?

The day came when the first of the children turned up at the house that had been requisitioned as a school. Four mothers arrived with six children. The eldest was eleven and the youngest six. Once they were registered I was allocated four of the oldest. Some furniture had been ordered, but had not arrived. My charges sat on the floor and I issued them with pencils and paper and began my first lesson with schoolchildren. I forget what I had planned to do with them. After a quarter of an hour, all the paper was used up and some of the pencils were broken, so I began to invent a story. Where was the major?

'I want my mummy,' cried the youngest.

'What can we do next?' said the eldest girl.

At that very moment the major arrived with refreshments.

'I don't like tea.'

'I don't like tea either. Can we have some orange juice?'

'Not today you can't,' replied the major. 'If you don't want tea, you can have water. I'll try to get orange cordial for you tomorrow.'

During the break two of the boys slipped upstairs to explore. They signalled their reappearance by sliding down the banisters. The more enterprising ascended to the second floor and slid down two sets of banisters. Soon all the children were sliding down two sets of banisters. Attempts to stop them by remonstrance were of no avail. This was a sport better than school lessons, and they had no wish to stop. Shouting had no effect. The major grabbed each one as he came down and stood each against the wall. Soon all were standing still by the wall. I had much to learn about controlling the behaviour of children. It is essential to retain the initiative. It is essential to anticipate each development and act accordingly. What initiative the major had up his sleeve I never knew, as at that moment there was the sound of a truck drawing up outside to take the children home. The driver came into the house and saw the children lined up by the wall. 'Come for the kids,' he said, 'Aren't the little blighters well behaved! How do you manage to do it, sir?'

Once the children were out of the building, the major roared with laughter. 'Well, that's a very good introduction to teaching for you. If only those who write books on the art of teaching could have been with us today. Now the first thing we have to do is to put wood blocks on the banisters to stop them sliding down them again.'

In fact I never did return to the school. The major decided to close it until desks had been installed, and by the time that had been accomplished I was home, never to return. I was called to the battery office near Christmas and told that my promotion to sergeant had come through, backdated a month. I asked the German tailor attached to our regiment to sew on my new stripes and then I reported back to the sergeants' mess. There the RSM greeted me and bought me a drink, as was the custom.

'I know you are being released tomorrow, but we must keep up the traditions. Yours must be the quickest promotion and release in the history of the regiment.' I was ill-at-ease in such lofty company. RSMs are a very special breed. They had the power to terrorise the rank and file, and the power to intimidate junior officers. I had never been on familiar terms with one before. Jumping up from lance-bombardier to sergeant was not an easy transition. I made my excuses and returned to my billet. It was not worthwhile transferring my gear to the mess for just one night.

My journey home began with a slow train from Oldenburg to Bremerhaven. It was slow because the track needed maintenance, and because the steam engines were old and exhausted. So much damage had been done to the German railway system, it was a wonder that trains were running at all, even eighteen months since the war ended. It was bitterly cold. There was no heating in the carriages. Men curled up as best they could to keep warm. I had my Army greatcoat and a leather jacket over my battledress, but the cold penetrated to the bone. At last we reached the port and stiffly clambered out onto the quayside. A piercing wind from the North Sea added to our chill. After some delay we climbed up the gangplank into the bowels of a Liberty ship and the heat within welcomed us. We rejoiced in the warmth of the ship. I had some men with me and held their 'demob' papers, which had to be produced on boarding. I handed them over to each man. Now it was every man for himself. I saw no reason to act as NCO in charge any longer.

Christmas card from the demobilising centre, received by the author as he collected his civilian clothes.

We found our bunks, not hammocks, and settled ourselves in. It was a twenty-four-hour journey from the German port to Hull. The sea was quite rough. The rise and fall of the ship as she ploughed through the bleak waters became more pronounced. This motion did not cause me any trouble, but when the ship began to roll heavily, I sought my bunk and fought off sea sickness. After a hard struggle to keep my food down I was sick into the newspaper I was carrying. I took no more food from the American-style servery on the rest of the voyage, but I did manage to enjoy and keep down some strong black coffee. Once ashore at Hull, we were all scrutinised by military police. I was carrying a large wooden box that I had had made by a carpenter in Berlin to contain a collection of gramophone records that I had bought cheaply there.

'What have you got in there, Sergeant?' said the senior policeman.

I explained what was within the box and how I had come by them.

'Step inside, sergeant.'

The case was opened, the contents examined. My backpack was opened and also examined. I realised they were looking for guns. There was a demand for guns brought back as trophies. The criminal underworld was hoping for rich pickings. All returning soldiers had been warned not to bring guns home. There were severe penalties for anyone caught smuggling weapons in. I recalled my near-fatal incident in the field the day the war ended. I had possessed an Italian revolver since then, but the night before I left the barracks I had walked to the river and thrown the pistol into the water and scattered the bullets in a nearby park.

'You will have to pay excise duty on those records,' I was told by a civilian clerk.

I forget what it was I had to pay on the spot, but I was highly indignant; the amount virtually wiped out any benefit I had accrued from having my Army pay backdated upon my promotion. Had it been worthwhile lugging those records home? Probably not. I had to invest in a gramophone, and I played them little.

Having passed through search and customs, I proceeded thought the docks into a large shed, where there was an extensive assembly of civilian clothing. I was allowed to pick up a suit, some shoes and socks, and fresh underwear. I chose a brown single-breasted suit. These articles were packed into a carrier bag and I made my way to a waiting train bound for London. I was handed a Christmas card from the demob centre as I left. It was a nice gesture, and I still have it. I elected to keep my greatcoat. I changed trains and got out at Sunnymeads Station on the Waterloo-Windsor line. I walked the mile to the bungalow in Wraysbury, where I had a surprise reunion with my mother. I was home just in time for Christmas 1946.

Postscript

In 1949 I received a letter from Anneliese saying that she was on a visit to England and would like to meet me again. She came to Wraysbury and gave my mother a little present. I was embarrassed. I was now courting a girl I was studying with at college. Did Anneliese have hopes of forming a relationship with me, or was it just a friendly visit for old times' sake? I made it clear that I was courting another, and we parted for ever. I wonder what became of her.

I qualified as a certificated teacher in 1950. I married Joan Newson, George's sister, in 1953. In 1990 she died, and after ten years on my own I married again, to Olive. My mother died in 1959. George Newson married a Flemish girl, Greta, and entered the Civil Service. Maurice Tyerman married Elsie from Leeds, and became an inspector of schools. He and I went to a reunion in Le Havre in 1989 to celebrate the forty-fifth anniversary of the siege and capitulation of that strongly defended city. I went again in 2004 with my son to celebrate the sixtieth anniversary. Maurice and I also went on Maj. Holt's battlefield tour to Normandy in 2002 and visited many of the places we had been associated with, including the war memorial to the 49th Polar Bear Division at the crossroad at Rauray.

Wally Coldrick became a teacher of art, and this year I had a telephone call from him. After all these years we found each other still alive. Dennis Bould went back to tailoring in Leeds. We met again several times after 1990, when I learned of the annual 274 Battery Reunion in Leeds. It no longer meets, as there are few survivors now.

The confirmation of George and me in Eindhoven by the Bishop of Dover had consequences. When George married Greta, from a small village in Brabant, he was received into the Roman Catholic Church. Greta could not consider marrying George without his becoming a Catholic. George was quite happy to do so. I was slowly drawn into the church. I began my teaching in a small church school, and little by little I became a regular Anglican. In 1984 I was licensed as a reader in the Diocese of Rochester, a position I held until I retired from the office in 2000.

Reflections

While stationed in Germany in my last year in the Army, I had 'Far East 1' entered in my pay book. This signified that I was fit to go to the Far East to carry on the war against the Japanese, a prospect I viewed with misgivings. It had been bad enough fighting the Germans, but at least they recognised the Red Cross and generally treated their prisoners fairly; the Japanese were known to be brutal and callous, even with the lives of their own soldiers, and recognised no Geneva Convention. I was not unhappy to hear that the Americans had dropped atomic bombs on Nagasaki and Hiroshima, and that Emperor Hirohito had surrendered. At last, the war was over everywhere. I do not recall celebrating the event, as I had the German surrender. I did not then feel sorry for the Japanese casualties, however horrific. I was just glad the war was over and I did not have to go east to continue the fight. Thoughts about the morality of dropping the 'A' bomb, and its implications for the future, came later.

My four-and-a-half years in the Army had been an experience I would not have missed for anything. Most us did not want to go to war, but there was a job to be done. Nazi Germany threatened our country. It was a brutal regime. Not until the war was over did we realise the full extent of its wickedness. I had experienced companionship and hardship. I had made lifelong friends. There was a good deal of boredom, punctuated by periods of intense activity and occasional great danger. I learned what loyalty and comradeship meant. I experienced the endurance and humour of the common soldier. What keeps you going in adversity is loyalty to your comrades. For many years I thought little about my war experiences. Most of my colleagues at Hurstmere Secondary School for Boys in Sidcup had served in the war. We all had a deep well of memories. But it was not done to talk about such things for a long time. Some have never done so. Some have bottled it up and possibly suffered some degree of mental illness. I could never bottle things up! My wife and my children have learned all about my war experiences.

A note on the author

John Mercer served in the Royal Artillery as a signaller from 1942 until 1947. Later he pursued a career in education, becoming a schoolteacher and then a college lecturer. He has also acted as chairman of the Bexley Civic Society and from 1969 to 2000 was a lay reader in the Diocese of Rochester.

He lives in Sidcup in the London Borough of Bexley and his previous books include *Mike Target, Sidcup: A Pictorial History*, *Bexley, Bexleyheath and Welling: A Pictorial History* and *The London Borough of Bexley, Chislehurst and Sidcup*. He has contributed to several military magazines and newsletters, including *The Gunner* and *The Polar Bear News*.

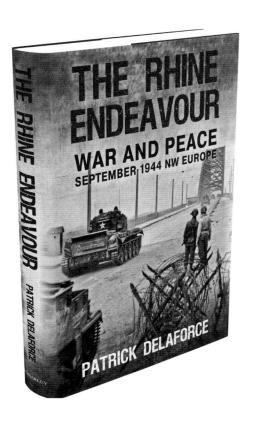

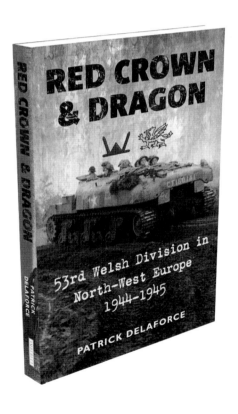

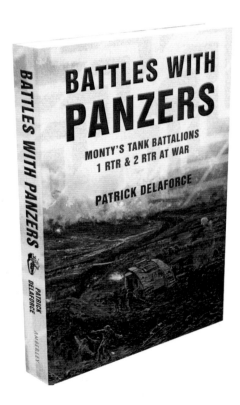